T0214499

Lecture Notes in Computer Science 11719

More information about this series at http://www.springer.com/series/7407

Pen-Chung Yew · Per Stenström ·
Junjie Wu · Xiaoli Gong · Tao Li (Eds.)

Advanced Parallel Processing Technologies

13th International Symposium, APPT 2019
Tianjin, China, August 15–16, 2019
Proceedings

 Springer

Editors
Pen-Chung Yew
University of Minnesota
Minneapolis, MN, USA

Per Stenström (iD)
Chalmers University of Technology
Gothenburg, Sweden

Junjie Wu (iD)
National University of Defense Technology
Changsha, China

Xiaoli Gong
Nankai University
Tianjin, China

Tao Li
Nankai University
Tianjin, China

ISSN 0302-9743   ISSN 1611-3349   (electronic)
Lecture Notes in Computer Science
ISBN 978-3-030-29610-0   ISBN 978-3-030-29611-7   (eBook)
https://doi.org/10.1007/978-3-030-29611-7

LNCS Sublibrary: SL1 – Theoretical Computer Science and General Issues

This Springer imprint is published by the registered company Springer Nature Switzerland AG
The registered company address is: Gewerbestrasse 11, 6330 Cham, Switzerland

Preface

The ever-increasing demand of parallel processing drives society to investigate new computer architecture and system software techniques. Following this trend, APPT 2019 broadly captured the recent advances in parallel architectures and systems, parallel software, parallel algorithms and neural network applications, etc., and provided an excellent forum for the presentation of research efforts and the exchange of viewpoints.

We would like to express our gratitude to all the colleagues who submitted papers and congratulate those whose papers were accepted. Following the success of its past twelve conference editions, APPT 2019 managed to provide a high-quality program for all attendees. The Program Committee (PC) decided to accept 11 papers. All submissions were reviewed by three PC members. There was also an online discussion stage to guarantee that consensus was reached for each submission.

We would like to thank the authors for submitting their work to APPT 2019, and we would also like to show our sincere appreciation to the PC members. The 30 PC members did an excellent job in returning high-quality reviews in time and engaging in a constructive online discussion. We would also like to thank the general chairs (Prof. Ke Gong and Prof. Xiangke Liao), the organization chairs (Prof. Tao Li, Prof. Dezun Dong, and Prof. Xiangfei Meng), and the publication chairs (Prof. Junjie Wu and Prof. Xiaoli Gong). Our thanks also go to Springer for their assistance in putting the proceedings together.

July 2019

Pen-Chung Yew
Per Stenström

Organization

APPT 2019 was organized by the China Computer Federation.

General Chairs

Ke Gong	Nankai University, China
Xiangke Liao	National University of Defense Technology, China

Steering Committee Chair

Yong Dou	National University of Defense Technology, China

Steering Committee

Zhenzhou Ji	Harbin Institute of Technology, China
Dongsheng Wang	Tsinghua University, China
Xingwei Wang	Northeastern University, China
Chenggang Wu	Institute of Computing Technology, Chinese Academy of Sciences, China
Gongxuan Zhang	Nanjing University of Science and Technology, China
Junjie Wu	National University of Defense Technology, China

Organization Chairs

Tao Li	Nankai University, China
Xiangfei Meng	National SuperComputer Center in Tianjin, China
Dezun Dong	National University of Defense Technology, China

Organization Committee

Hong An	University of Science and Technology of China, China
Qiang Cao	Huazhong University of Science and Technology, China
Yunji Chen	Institute of Computing Technology, Chinese Academy of Sciences, China
Yun Liang	Peking University, China
Kuanjiu Zhou	Dalian University of Technology, China
Sonwen Pei	University of Shanghai for Science and Technology, China
Tian Song	Beijing Institute of Technology, China

Guanxue Yue   Jiangxi University of Science and Technology, China
Lifang Wen   China Machine Press, Beijing Huazhang Graphics
                                   & Information Co. Ltd., China

Program Chairs

Pen-Chung Yew   University of Minnesota, USA
Per Stenström   Chalmers University of Technology, Sweden

Program Committee

Manuel E. Acacio   University of Murcia, Spain
Trevor E. Carlson   National University of Singapore, Singapore
Paul Carpenter   Barcelona Supercomputing Center, Spain
Yong Chen   Texas Tech University, USA
Rudolf Eigenmann   University of Delaware, USA
Zhenman Fang   Simon Fraser University, Canada
Bok-Min Goi   Universiti Tunku Abdul Rahman, Malaysia
Anup Holey   Nvidia, USA
Guoliang Jin   North Carolina State University, USA
Jangwoo Kim   Seoul National University, South Korea
John Kim   Korea Advanced Institute of Science and Technology,
                                   South Korea
Zhiyuan Li   Purdue University, USA
Chen Liu   Clarkson University, USA
Lei Liu   Institute of Computing Technology, Chinese Academy
                                   of Sciences, China
Vassilis Papaefstathiou   FORTH-ICS, Greece
Miquel Pericas   Chalmers University of Technology, Sweden
Cristina Silvano   Politecnico di Milano, Italy
Magnus Själander   Norwegian University of Science and Technology,
                                   Norway
Shuaiwen Song   Pacific Northwest National Lab, USA
James Tuck   North Carolina State University, USA
Nian-Feng Tzeng   Center for Advanced Computer Studies,
                                   University of Louisiana at Lafayette, USA
Hans Vandierendonck   Queen's University Belfast, UK
Bo Wu   Colorado School of Mines, USA
Liao Xiaofei   Huazhong University of Science and Technology,
                                   China
Zhibin Yu   Shenzhen Institute of Advanced Technology, China
Mohamed Zahran   New York University, USA
Antonia Zhai   University of Minnesota, USA
Jidong Zhai   Tsinghua University, China
Weihua Zhang   Fudan University, China
Huiyang Zhou   NC State University, USA

Publicity and Exhibition Chairs

Weixing Ji   Beijing Institute of Technology, China
Jizeng Wei   Tianjin University, China

Publication Chairs

Junjie Wu   National University of Defense Technology, China
Xiaoli Gong   Nankai University, China

Workshop Chairs

Chao Li   Shanghai Jiaotong University, China
Lifang Wen   China Machine Press, Beijing Huazhang Graphics
                                      & Information Co. Ltd., China

Local Chair

Ye Lu   Nankai University, China

Poster Chair

Yong Xie   Xiamen University of Technology, China

Contents

System Support for Neural Networks

RV-CNN: Flexible and Efficient Instruction Set for CNNs Based
on RISC-V Processors 3
    Wenqi Lou, Chao Wang, Lei Gong, and Xuehai Zhou

Compiling Optimization for Neural Network Accelerators 15
    Jin Song, Yimin Zhuang, Xiaobing Chen, Tian Zhi, and Shaoli Liu

ZhuQue: A Neural Network Programming Model Based on Labeled
Data Layout 27
    Weijian Du, Linyang Wu, Xiaobing Chen, Yimin Zhuang, and Tian Zhi

Scheduling and File Systems

Reducing Rename Overhead in Full-Path-Indexed File System 43
    Longhua Wang, Youyou Lu, Siyang Li, Fan Yang, and Jiwu Shu

Partition and Scheduling Algorithms for Neural Network Accelerators 55
    Xiaobing Chen, Shaohui Peng, Luyang Jin, Yimin Zhuang, Jin Song,
    Weijian Du, Shaoli Liu, and Tian Zhi

Optimization and Parallelization

SPART: Optimizing CNNs by Utilizing Both Sparsity of Weights
and Feature Maps 71
    Jiaming Xie and Yun Liang

DA-BERT: Enhancing Part-of-Speech Tagging of Aspect Sentiment
Analysis Using BERT 86
    Songwen Pei, Lulu Wang, Tianma Shen, and Zhong Ning

Random Inception Module and Its Parallel Implementation 96
    Yingqi Gao, Kunpeng Xie, Song Guo, Kai Wang, Hong Kang,
    and Tao Li

Security and Algorithms

CBA-Detector: An Accurate Detector Against Cache-Based Attacks
Using HPCs and Pintools 109
    Beilei Zheng, Jianan Gu, and Chuliang Weng

An Efficient Log Parsing Algorithm Based on Heuristic Rules   123
   Lin Zhang, Xueshuo Xie, Kunpeng Xie, Zhi Wang, Ye Lu,
   and Yujun Zhang

Distribution Forest: An Anomaly Detection Method Based
on Isolation Forest   135
   Chengfei Yao, Xiaoqing Ma, Biao Chen, Xiaosong Zhao, and Gang Bai

Author Index   149

System Support for Neural Networks

RV-CNN: Flexible and Efficient Instruction Set for CNNs Based on RISC-V Processors

Wenqi Lou, Chao Wang$^{(\boxtimes)}$, Lei Gong, and Xuehai Zhou

School of Computer Science, University of Science and Technology of China,
Hefei, China
{louwenqi,leigong0203}@mail.ustc.edu.cn, {cswang,xhzhou}@ustc.edu.cn

Abstract. Convolutional Neural Network (CNN) has gained significant attention in the field of machine learning, particularly due to its high accuracy in character recognition and image classification. Nevertheless, due to the computation-intensive and memory-intensive character of CNN, general-purpose processors which usually need to support various workloads are not efficient for CNN implementation. Therefore, a great deal of emerging CNN-specific hardware accelerators is able to improve efficiency. Although existing accelerators are significantly efficient, they are often inflexible or require complex controllers to handle calculations and data transfer. In this paper, we analyze classical CNN applications and design a domain-specific instruction set of 9 matrix instructions, called RV-CNN, based on the promising RISC-V architecture. By abstracting CNN into instructions, our design possesses a higher code density and provides sufficient flexibility and efficiency for CNN than general-purpose ISAs. Specifically, the proposed instructions are extended to RISC-V ISA as custom instructions. Besides, we also introduce micro-architectural optimizations to increase computational density and reduce the required memory bandwidth. Finally, we implement the architecture with the extended ISA and evaluate it with LeNet-5 on the datasets (MNIST, Caltech101, and Cifar-10). Results show that compared with the Intel Core i7 processor and Tesla k40c GPU, our design has 36.09x and 11.42x energy efficiency ratio and 6.70x and 1.25x code density respectively.

Keywords: CNN · RISC-V · Domain-specific instructions · FPGA

1 Introduction

Convolutional neural network (CNN), a category of feed-forward artificial neural networks, is well known for its high precision in the fields of character recognition, image classification, and face detection [10,13,14]. Inspired by the visual cortex of the brain, CNN is typically composed of multi-layer networks. In recent years, with the improvement of recognition accuracy, the depth of the network

© Springer Nature Switzerland AG 2019
P.-C. Yew et al. (Eds.): APPT 2019, LNCS 11719, pp. 3–14, 2019.
https://doi.org/10.1007/978-3-030-29611-7_1

has been considerably increased. However, a deeper network structure means more computation and more weight data access, which makes the low efficiency of general-purpose processors in performing CNN calculations intolerable. Therefore, various accelerators based on FPGA [8,15,16], GPU [9], and ASIC [2] have been proposed, which gain better performance than general-purpose processors. However, these accelerators are often optimized only for some layers of the neural network, with less flexibility. To address this problem, Chen's team proposes Cambricon [11], a domain-specific Instruction Set Architecture (ISA) for NN accelerators, which supports ten network structures and has higher code density and performance than traditional ISA. Nevertheless, it is not specific to CNNs, thereby overlooking the reusability and parallelism of data. Flexible for CNNs, DaDianNao [3] can support the Multi-Layer Perceptrons (MLPs), but it demands substantial reconfigurable computing units and complex control. In [5,6], Luca et al. propose a Hardware Convolution Engine (HWCE) based on RISC-V architecture and achieve significant results, but they only design instructions for convolution operation, without considering other layers. Thus, an efficient and flexible CNN-specific instruction set is still demanding.

In this paper, we present a novel lightweight ISA for CNN reference, called RV-CNN. It consists of 9 instructions based on RISC-V, thereby to support the current mainstream CNN technologies. The main work of this paper is summarized as follows:

- Though studying computational patterns of the popular CNNs, we propose a small and easy-to-implement CNN-specific instruction set, which can flexibly support a variety of CNN structures.
- Breaking the traditional peripheral accelerator pattern, we extend CNN-specific instructions into RISC-V five-stage pipeline architecture and particularly optimize the implementation of instructions.
- As a case study, we implement our design and evaluate it from code density, performance, and power consumption, which demonstrates our design possess promising energy efficiency.

The rest of this paper is organized as follows. Section 2 briefly introduces our motivations and a few design preferences. Section 3 describes the details of the new ISA. Section 4 illustrates the overall architecture. Section 5 displays the experiment setup and evaluation results. Section 6 is the conclusion.

2   Motivations and Preferences

2.1   Motivations

Flexibility. Although compared with general-purpose processors, application scenarios that hardware accelerators for CNNs will deal with are much decreased and more certain, there are still many network structures which are different but have similarities, possessing different strengths. Nevertheless, common hardware accelerators normally deploy the whole or part of the neural network on the

FPGA, in which the network structure is often not reconfigured due to time expense. Thus, we expect to provide more flexibility for CNN techniques by abstracting the intensive operations in CNNs into dedicated instructions. Users can write assembly instructions to build a particular CNN.

Efficiency. Typically, an accelerator serves as a peripheral to the host CPU. Hence, the host CPU is in charge of transferring data from the main memory to the accelerator over a bus. It is obviously not a negligible overhead because of additional processing in the operating system and massive data. Besides, bus bandwidth also limits the performance of these accelerators. Therefore, instead of the previous pattern, we deploy the acceleration unit into the processor's pipeline, and then optimize the memory access of the acceleration unit to satisfy its data bandwidth requirements, thereby improving efficiency.

2.2 Design Preferences

RISC-V Extension. Designing a completely novel CNN-specific ISA usually involves plenty of factors, but the part that restricts the speed of calculation is what matters precisely. In view of the extensibility of RISC-V, we extend it with our dedicated instructions which are crucial to accelerating the CNN computing, while maintaining the basic kernel and each standard extension unchanged. In this way, we can concentrate on designing our CNN instructions, as well as directly using scalar and logical control instructions that the RISC-V provides. Moreover, we can also utilize the toolchain provided by RISC-V to speed up the development process.

Data-Level Parallelism. Taking the topological structure of convolutional neural networks (layer-by-layer) and the independence of weight matrices between layers into account, it is a more efficient way that utilizes data-level parallelism by applying matrix instructions than exploring instruction-level parallelism in NN operations. Furthermore, when dealing with calculations involving large amounts of data, matrix instructions can explicitly specify the independence between the data blocks, which can significantly reduce the size of dependency detection logic, compared to the conventional scalar instructions. What's more, matrix instructions also possess higher code density, so we chiefly focus on data-level parallelism here.

Scratchpad Memory. Vector registers commonly appear in the vector architecture, each of which is a fixed-length bank holding a single vector, and allow processors to operate all elements in a vector at one time. Scratchpad memory [1], a high-speed internal memory used for the temporary storage of calculations, can be accessed by direct addressing, costs low power, and supports variable-length data accesses. Considering that dense, continuous, variable-length data access often occurs in CNNs, and weight data rarely reused, we replace vector registers with the scratchpad memory in our design.

3   Details of Custom Instructions

3.1   Custom Instructions

We design the RV-CNN architecture, including both data transfer and computational instructions, as shown in Table 1. Cooperating with the base ISA, RV-CNN can perform typical CNN calculations. RV-CNN has 32 32-bit General-Purpose Registers, which can be used to store scalar values, as well as in register-indirect addressing of the on-chip scratchpad memory. Additionally, due to the 32-bit instruction length limit, we set up a vector length register (VLR) to ascertain the length of the vector, similar to the vector architecture. RV-CNN still access memory only through the corresponding MLOAD/MSTORE, obeying a load-store architecture of RISC-V. The instructions already in RISC-V are not described here.

Table 1. An overview of RV-CNN.

Instruction type	Example
Data Transfer	MLOAD/MSTORE
Computational	MMM/MSIG/MSFMX/MRELU
Logical	MAXPOOL/MINPOOL/APOOL

Data Transfer Instructions. To flexibly support matrix operations, data transfer instructions can load/store variable-size data blocks (an integer multiple of VLR value) from/to main memory. Specifically, the stride field of instructions can designate the stride of adjacent elements, avoiding expensive matrix transpose operations in memory. Figure 1 illustrates the matrix load (MLOAD) instruction, where Reg0 specifies the destination address; Reg1, Reg2, and Reg3 respectively specify the source address of matrix, the size of the matrix, and the stride of adjacent elements. Matrix store (MSTORE) instruction is similar to that of MLOAD, while regularly ignoring the stride fields.

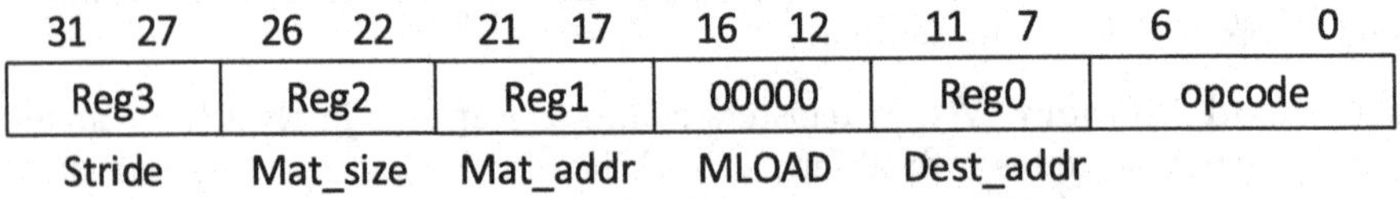

31 27	26 22	21 17	16 12	11 7	6 0
Reg3	Reg2	Reg1	00000	Reg0	opcode
Stride	Mat_size	Mat_addr	MLOAD	Dest_addr	

Fig. 1. Matrix Load (MLOAD) instruction.

Matrix Computational Instructions. CNNs are mainly composed of convolutional layers, pooling layers, and fully-connected layers, where the most computation concentrates in convolutional layers [4]. In the convolutional layer, convolution kernels move continuously on input feature maps and do a dot-product operation with the coincidence region to generate the input data of the next layer. Nevertheless, in this process, the operation between different feature maps and corresponding convolution kernels is independent of each other. To make full use of data parallelism, we adopt mapping technology (im2col algorithm) to transform 3-D convolution operation to MM operation (see Fig. 2 for an illustration). Moreover, the computing unit can be reused by fully-connected layers on account of analogous MM (row = 1) computing pattern. Note that instead of storing the entire input feature data, the rearrangement is performed before when we store them in the FPGA on-chip memory.

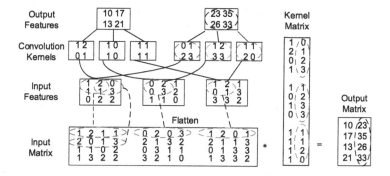

Fig. 2. Matrix multiplication version of convolution.

After mapping the 3D convolution to MM (matrix multiplication) operation, we use the Matrix-Mult-Matrix instruction to perform it. It is illustrated in Fig. 3, where Reg0 specifies the base scratchpad memory address of the matrix output (Destination address); Inst[16:12] is the function field of the instruction, indicating the MM operation. Reg1 and Reg2 specify the base address of the matrix1 and matrix2 respectively. The upper 16 bits and the lower 16 bits in Reg3 specify the number of rows of matrix 1 and the number of columns of matrix 2 (Rows + Cols), respectively. Accordingly, the size of matrix1 and matrix2 can be ascertained by the value in VLR and Reg3. To utilize greater extent of data locality as well as reduce concurrent read/write requests to the same address, we choose to adopt dedicated the MMM instruction to perform matrix multiplication instead of decomposing it into finer-grained instruction (e.g., matrix-mult-vector and vector dot products) here.

31 27	26 22	21 17	16 12	11 7	6 0
Reg3	Reg2	Reg1	00010	Reg0	opcode
R+C	Mat2_addr	Mat1_addr	MMM	Dest_addr	

Fig. 3. Matrix Multiply Matrix (MMM) instruction.

The Matrix Sigmoid (MSIG) and the Matrix Softmax (MSFMX) instruction are essential to complete the entire computation. By default, we employ the MSIG instruction to activate the input data through the sigmoid function, to define the output of neurons. Alternatively, users can choose the MRELU or MTANH instruction to implement the relu or the tanh function by modifying the Inst [31:27] field (see Fig. 4). Correspondingly, to obtain the prediction results, the MSFMX instruction is used to normalize the output data.

31 27	26 22	21 17	16 12	11 7	6 0
Reg3	Reg2	Reg1	00110	Reg0	opcode
MSIG	Mat_size	Mat_addr	Activate	Dest_addr	

Fig. 4. Matrix Sigmoid (MSIG) Instruction.

Matrix Logical Instruction. The formats of maximum pooling (MAXPOOL) instruction (see Fig. 5) are similar to those of MLOAD, where reg0, reg1, and reg2 possess the same meaning as MLOAD instruction, respectively presenting destination address of output data, source address, and size of the input matrix. Whereas, as to the GPOOL instruction, the upper 16 bits and the lower 16 bits in Reg3 respectively designate the size and sliding step of kernels. Also, the MINPOOL (minimum pooling) or APOOL (average pooling) instruction, only differing from the function field of the MAXPOOL instruction, can be taken to determine the minimum or average pooling.

31 27	26 22	21 17	16 12	11 7	6 0
Reg3	Reg2	Reg1	00100	Reg0	opcode
K+S	Mat_size	Mat_addr	MAXPOOL	Dest_addr	

Fig. 5. Maximum Pooling (MAXPOOL) instruction.

3.2   Code Examples

To illustrate the usage of our proposed instructions, we implement two simple yet representative components of CNN, a convolutional layer and a pooling layer. The example code of the fully-connected layer is similar to that of the convolutional layer, except that the output should pass through the activation function.

Convolutional Layer Code:

```
//$1:input mat1 address, $2:input mat2 address
//$3:temp variable address, $4:output size
//$5:row of mat1, col of mat2, $6:mat1 address, $7:mat1 size
//$8:mat2 address, $9:mat2 size, $10:output matrix address
    LI       $5,    0x0310_0006 //row of mat1(784),col of mat2(6)
    LI       $VLR, 0x1A         //set vector length(26)
    MLOAD    $1, $6, $7         //load kernel matrix
    MLOAD    $2, $8, $9         //load feature map matrix
    MMM      $3, $2, $1, $5     //mat1 x mat2
    MSTORE   $3, $10, $4        //store output to address($10)
```

Pooling Layer Code:

```
//$1:input mat address, $2:feature map size
//$3:loop counter, $4~$6:temp variable address
//$8:mat address, $7:output mat address, $9:output size
       ADDI     $4, $6, #0
       LI       $10,   0x0004_0002 //kernel size:2x2,step=2
       LI       $VLR, 0x1C         //set vector length(28)
       LI       $3,    0x06        //set loop counter(6)
L0:MLOAD $1, $8, $2                //load feature map
       APOOL    $5, $1, $2, $10    //subsample
       MSIG     $4, $5, $2         //activate
       ADDI     $4, $4, 0xC4       //update temp address(add 14x14)
       ADD      $8, $8, $2         //next feature map
       SUB      $3, $3, #1
       BGE      $3, #0, L0         //if(loop counter>0) goto label0
       MSTORE   $6, $7, $9         //store mat to address($7)
```

4 Implementation Details

4.1 Overall Architecture

A simplified block diagram of the RV-CNN core architecture displaying its pipeline stages and major functional blocks is illustrated in Fig. 6. It includes five stages: fetching, decoding, execution, memory access, and write-back, in which the matrix computing unit is in the execution stage of the pipeline. Since the matrix unit can directly interact with the scratchpad memory, matrix operations do not go through the memory access and write-back stage. Correspondingly, after the fetching and decoding stage, the instructions in the base ISA will enter the ALU then go to the next stage, while the custom instructions will perform corresponding operations such as data transmission, convolution, and activation through the matrix unit. The address space of the scratchpad memory is mapped to the main memory by global mapping, and the remaining memory address space is still accessed through the cache. We can readily embed Direct Memory Access (DMA) in the matrix unit for the data transfer.

Furthermore, through appending a data buffer between the matrix unit and the scratchpad memory, we can effectively reduce the data delay. In a nutshell, the scratchpad memory and cache are relatively independent, and the control module will detect the data dependence and decide whether to stall the pipeline or not. By default, data involved in the execution of matrix computational logical instructions should already exist in the scratchpad memory, which requires strict control from the program.

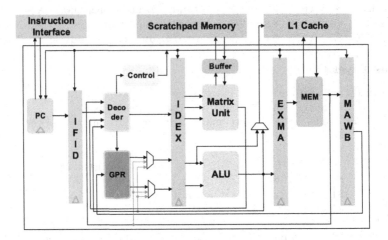

Fig. 6. A simplified block diagram of the RV-CNN core.

4.2   Matrix Unit's Architecture

The overall structure of the matrix unit is illustrated in Fig. 7, where the orange and black arrows represent the control flow and the data flow, respectively. As we can see, the internal controller, which works as a finite state machine, is the center of the matrix unit. After receiving control signals from the previous stage, the controller arouses the sub-component to complete the corresponding task if it is available. Otherwise, it will generate a feedback signal to indicate that the task is busy. The matrix unit contains four sub-units: Matrix multiplication, Sigmoid, Pooling, and Softmax. The buffer module is essentially an on-chip memory that buffers the input and output matrices and temporarily stores intermediate results. Lastly, the input/output module is responsible for receiving/sending the elements of the matrix in order.

4.3   Optimization

Since we reuse the MM unit to complete the computation-intensive convolutional layers and memory-intensive fully-connected layers, the performance of the MM unit exerts a significant impact on that of the whole matrix unit. Therefore, we adopt an adder tree and data reuse to optimize the MM unit in terms of computation and data access (see Fig. 7).

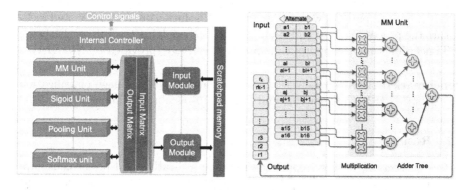

Fig. 7. The architecture of matrix unit (left); Optimizing details for MM Unit (right).

Adder tree. Matrix multiplication composes of multiple vector dot products where the length of the vector is variably regulated by VLR. In our design, the length of two vectors that MM unit to handle is fixed at 16. Therefore, vector length greater than 16 will be fragmented, and less than 16 will be padded with zeros. We deploy several DSP48Es to complete the float-point addition and multiplication and optimize the accumulation process of the dot product by adopting a binary tree, which significantly reduces the time complexity, from $O(N)$ to $O(\log N)$. At the same time, utilizing pipeline technology, we can get sum or partial sum in every clock cycle.

Data reuse. After the data required for matrix multiplication has been transferred from the main memory to the scratchpad memory, the matrix unit continuously acquires two vectors through the input unit to complete computing. Considering the potential data locality in multiplication calculation, we lessen data bandwidth requirements through data reuse. Clearly, the reuse distance of the feature data is quite shorter than that of the weight matrix. Hence, we give priority to the reuse of the feature matrix. Meanwhile, we set two vectors to read the weight data, alternately used in current iteration computation.

5   Experiment and Results

5.1   Experiment Method

Platform. We synthesize the prototype system, then place, route the synthesized design in Vivado 2017.4, and evaluate the core by deploying it in Nexys4 DDR development board.

Baselines. We compare the performance of our system with existing implementations on general-purpose CPU and GPU.

– CPU. The CPU baseline is i7-4790K. We compare the processing time and power of our design with those of the CPU version of the program, utilizing the PAPI (Performance Application Programming Interface) tool which is an open source project provided by Intel, and gettimeofday() function.

– GPU. For comparison, we implement a GPU solution on Tesla k40c, and measure the processing time and running power by applying the cuEventElapsedTime() function and nvprof command respectively (provided by NVIDIA).

Benchmarks. Based on LeNet-5, we take three common image classification data sets (MNIST, CalTech 101, and CIFAR-10) as our benchmarks.

5.2 Results

In this subsection, we first report the resource utilization and power consumption of the system in the FPGA board, and then compare our design on the FPGA with CPU, GPU, and existing FPGA-based accelerators in three aspects respectively.

Area and power. We obtain the utilization of resources and the power consumption of FPGA by checking the implementation report in Vivado tools (LUT: 39.09%, 24780; FF: 26.49%, 33594; BRAM: 21.85%, 29.5; DSP: 50.42%, 121; and Power: 0.331 W).

Flexibility. The dedicated ISA we propose is not only suitable for accelerating CNN applications but also provides support to other deep learning algorithms with similar computing patterns, like DNNs. We implement the popular CNNs (Lenet-5, Alexnet, VGG) by using the specific instructions and measure the average code size of three CNNs. Compared with the GPU, x86, and MIPS, RV-CNN achieves 1.25x, 6.70x, 9.51x reduction of code length respectively.

Energy Efficiency. We compare the energy consumption of our system with CPU and GPU in the CNN reference process. As shown in the Fig. 8, the power consumption of CPU and GPU is 91.03x and 228.66x that of our design, and the energy consumption is 36.09x and 11.42x that of our design, respectively. Experimental results indicate that our design is significantly better than CPU and GPU in terms of energy consumption.

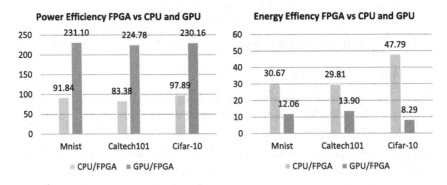

Fig. 8. Power ratios (left) and Energy ratios (right) vs CPU and GPU (Based on LeNet-5).

Performance. We also compare our design with the existing accelerators. Since different work adopts different quantization strategies and platforms, it is hard to choose a precise and effective comparison method. As we can see, taking Giga Operations Per Second (GOPS) as the evaluation standard, previous works can achieve better performance than ours. However, higher performance is the consumption of more resources, such as DSP blocks. In view of efficiency, we finally chose a relatively fair comparison standard - performance/w, which is defined as average GOPS per watt. As shown in Table 2, compared to previous works, our design achieves the highest performance efficiency.

Table 2. Comparison with other FPGA accelerators.

	[7]	[17]	[12]	Ours
Platform	Zynq XC7Z045	Virtex7 VX485T	Zynq XC7Z045	Artix7 XC7A100T
Frequency(MHz)	150	100	150	100
Precision	16-bit fixed	32-bit float	Q15	32-bit float
Power(W)	8	18.61	10	0.331
Perf(GOPS)	23.18	61.62	38.4	3.14(CONV)
DSP util	N/A	2240	391	121
Perf/w(GOPS/w)	2.90	3.31	3.84	9.48

6   Conclusion

In this work, we present an easy-to-implement CNN-specific instruction set, called RV-CNN, to provide more flexibility for CNN structures. Through studying computational patterns of the popular CNN techniques, we design nine coarse-grained matrix instructions in RV-CNN and extend the base RISC-V ISA with it. Then, we embed the corresponding acceleration unit in the classic five-stage pipeline architecture. Using Xilinx Artix7 100T to implement our design, compared with the Intel Core i7 processor and Tesla k40c GPU, it holds 36.09x and 11.42x energy efficiency ratio and 6.70x and 1.25x code density respectively. Besides, compared with the existing accelerators, it also achieves a promising energy efficiency.

Acknowledgments. This work is partially supported by the National Key Research and Development Program of China (under Grant 2017YFA0700900), National Science Foundation of China (No. 61772482), Jiangsu Provincial Natural Science Foundation (No. BK20181193), Youth Innovation Promotion Association CAS (No. 2017497), and Fundamental Research Funds for the Central Universities (WK2150110003).

References

1. Banakar, R., Steinke, S., Lee, B.S., Balakrishnan, M., Marwedel, P.: Scratchpad memory: a design alternative for cache on-chip memory in embedded systems. In: International Symposium on Hardware/software Codesign (2002)

2. Chen, T., et al.: DianNao: a small-footprint high-throughput accelerator for ubiquitous machine-learning. In: ACM SIGPLAN Notices, vol. 49, pp. 269–284. ACM (2014)
3. Chen, Y., Luo, T., Liu, S., Zhang, S., He, L., et al.: DaDianNao: a machine-learning supercomputer. In: Proceedings of the 47th Annual IEEE/ACM International Symposium on Microarchitecture, pp. 609–622. IEEE Computer Society (2014)
4. Cong, J., Xiao, B.: Minimizing computation in convolutional neural networks. In: Wermter, S., et al. (eds.) ICANN 2014. LNCS, vol. 8681, pp. 281–290. Springer, Cham (2014). https://doi.org/10.1007/978-3-319-11179-7_36
5. Conti, F., Rossi, D., Pullini, A., Loi, I., Benini, L.: PULP: a ultra-low power parallel accelerator for energy-efficient and flexible embedded vision. J. Signal Process. Syst. **84**(3), 339–354 (2016)
6. Flamand, E., et al.: GAP-8: a RISC-V SoC for AI at the edge of the IoT. In: 2018 IEEE 29th International Conference on Application-Specific Systems, Architectures and Processors (ASAP), pp. 1–4. IEEE (2018)
7. Gokhale, V., Jin, J., Dundar, A., Martini, B., Culurciello, E.: A 240 G-ops/s mobile coprocessor for deep neural networks. In: Proceedings of the IEEE Conference on Computer Vision and Pattern Recognition Workshops, pp. 682–687 (2014)
8. Gong, L., Wang, C., Li, X., Chen, H., Zhou, X.: MALOC: a fully pipelined fpga accelerator for convolutional neural networks with all layers mapped on chip. IEEE Trans. Comput.-Aided Des. Integr. Circuits Syst. **37**(11), 2601–2612 (2018)
9. Krizhevsky, A., Sutskever, I., Hinton, G.E.: ImageNet classification with deep convolutional neural networks. In: Advances in Neural Information Processing Systems, pp. 1097–1105 (2012)
10. LeCun, Y., Bottou, L., Bengio, Y., Haffner, P., et al.: Gradient-based learning applied to document recognition. Proc. IEEE **86**(11), 2278–2324 (1998)
11. Liu, S., et al.: Cambricon: an instruction set architecture for neural networks. In: ACM SIGARCH Computer Architecture News, vol. 44, pp. 393–405. IEEE Press (2016)
12. Moini, S., Alizadeh, B., Ebrahimpour, R.: A resource-limited hardware accelerator for convolutional neural networks in embedded vision applications. IEEE Trans. Circuits Syst. II: Express Briefs **64**(10), 1217–1221 (2017)
13. Simonyan, K., Zisserman, A.: Very deep convolutional networks for large-scale image recognition. arXiv preprint arXiv:1409.1556 (2014)
14. Sun, Y., Chen, Y., Wang, X., Tang, X.: Deep learning face representation by joint identification-verification. In: Advances in Neural Information Processing Systems, pp. 1988–1996 (2014)
15. Wang, C., Gong, L., Yu, Q., Li, X., Xie, Y., Zhou, X.: DLAU: a scalable deep learning accelerator unit on FPGA. IEEE Trans. Comput.-Aided Des. Integr. Circuits Syst. **36**(3), 513–517 (2016)
16. Wang, C., Li, X., Chen, Y., Zhang, Y., Diessel, O., Zhou, X.: Service-oriented architecture on FPGA-based MPSoC. IEEE Trans. Parallel Distrib. Syst. **28**(10), 2993–3006 (2017)
17. Zhang, C., Li, P., Sun, G., Guan, Y., Xiao, B., Cong, J.: Optimizing FPGA-based accelerator design for deep convolutional neural networks. In: Proceedings of the 2015 ACM/SIGDA International Symposium on Field-Programmable Gate Arrays, pp. 161–170. ACM (2015)

Compiling Optimization for Neural Network Accelerators

Jin Song[1,2,3(✉)], Yimin Zhuang[1,2,3], Xiaobing Chen[1,2,3],
Tian Zhi[2,3(✉)], and Shaoli Liu[2,3]

[1] University of Chinese Academy of Sciences, Beijing, China
[2] SKL of Computer Architecture, Institute of Computing Technology, CAS,
Beijing, China
{songjin, zhitian}@ict.ac.cn
[3] Cambricon Tech. Ltd., Beijing, China

Abstract. Nowadays artificial neural networks are one of the most common computational models among all the intelligent methods. To cope with the ever-growing scales of neural networks and the restrictions of system energy consumption, there comes out a bunch of neural network (NN) accelerators. However, owing to their dedicated architecture, programming on NN accelerators is different from general processors. In order to improve performance, it is necessary to use global structure information of NN model to optimize the compilation. In this paper, we introduce a series of layer-based compile optimizations for NN accelerators. From top to bottom, we define a type of computational graph, carrying necessary information such as relationship between layer nodes and data nodes. Then according to the pattern of a NN layer computation process, we apply an intra layer loop unrolling and pipelining, including fine-grained and coarse-grained two levels. Similarly, we apply layer fusion optimization based on our computational graph and abstract pipelining stage. After expanding pipelining stages of layers, we can reduce some redundant IO operations, which we call it layer elimination optimization. The experiment results show that with our proposed optimizations the inference process can achieve up to 1.34x speedup than not using fusion optimization.

Keywords: Neural network accelerator · Compile optimization · Layer fusion

1 Introduction

At present, intelligent applications such as image recognition [1–3], target detection [4, 5] and natural language processing [6, 7] have become one of the hottest spots both in commercial and research areas. Artificial Intelligence (AI) are not only used in a lot of smart applications but even in the complex strategy games like Go [8, 9], Dota2 [10]. To some extent, AI has started to beat human in the man-machine matches.

However, as the deep learning algorithm is highly intensive in computation and memory access, the traditional processors can no longer meet the demand of intelligent applications. For instance, in the field of intelligent driving, the forward inference operations have strict sequential requirements. In this context, lots of machine learning

© Springer Nature Switzerland AG 2019
P.-C. Yew et al. (Eds.): APPT 2019, LNCS 11719, pp. 15–26, 2019.
https://doi.org/10.1007/978-3-030-29611-7_2

accelerators have come out [11–15, 17, 18]. Theory and practice have proved that, using dedicated intelligent processor to accelerate machine learning algorithm, the energy efficiency ratio can be improved dozens or even hundreds of times compared to the general processors. In practical applications, most of the NN accelerators adopt verified methods (e.g. low-precision representation, quantitative calculation, sparse weights, ReLU (Rectified Linear Unit) layer and so on) to acquire performance improvement. And there is also an Instruction Set Architecture (ISA) for NN [19] proposed for the flexibility and effectiveness. However, those different optimizations bring complexity for NN compilation.

While programming on a NN accelerator, manual optimization for the whole network structure is unpractical because both the scale and the parameters in NNs are massive and complexity is exponentially-growing [20, 21, 23]. Moreover, the calculation methods in NN models are also changing with the development of algorithms. For example, dilated convolution layer adds a new parameter "dilation" to expand the receptive field [24]. They change the kernel data fetching orders. For AlexNet [1], there is group convolution structure; For MobileNet [25], there is depth separable convolution (Depth-wise Conv) structure; For ShuffleNet [3], the convolution layer follows shuffle layer, etc. Due to the complexity of NN algorithms and the deepening of models, the programming and optimization for NN accelerators must be automatically accomplished by software not by human programmer.

There are several popular deep learning frameworks (such as Tensorflow [27], caffe [28], MXNet [29], etc.) for AI developers to build their models and train, fine-tune and share to other researchers. However, the description of a model is usually expressed by operators or layers as basic units. Thus, we use a layer-based computing graph model as a high-level intermediate representation (IR) to optimize compilation. Subsequently, the low-level optimization is also based on layers. We propose a novel programming style called stage level parallel, taking advantage of NN accelerators instructions parallel execution on different types of on-chip resources. In inference process, some of parameters and scale of NN layers are constant and we can implement intra layer pipelining and loop unrolling to reduce redundant instructions. Also, between layers, based on stage level parallel instruction blocks, we can deploy layer fusion and layer elimination optimizations to get a further better performance.

2   Compiling Optimization

2.1   Definition of Computational Graph

We choose a high-level IR of optimization similar to that in TVM [34] where a node represents an operation and edges represent data dependencies between operations. Our graph uses nodes with a label of name represent layers and data which are linking in a layer as shown on the Fig. 1 below.

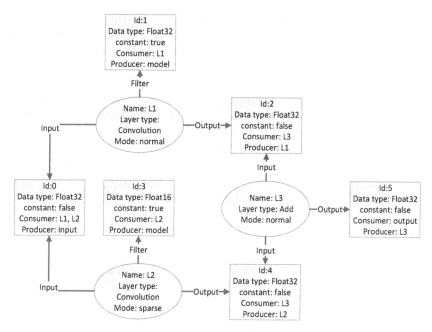

Fig. 1. Nodes information of computation graph. Rectangles represent data nodes and ovals represent layer nodes. Lines with arrows show the relationship index of a layer-data node pair.

For example, a convolution layer L1 receives user's input image as the input data for its computation and its output data is the input data of L3 (as shown in Fig. 1). Besides data nodes index, layer nodes attributes include more information such as identification number, layer types, computation mode, etc. Data nodes contain tags of off-chip memory allocation type, is constant or not, data type and so on.

And there is a more important information is the relationship of a layer-data node pair. We choose a producer-consumer model to describe dependencies between nodes. A layer node can have zero-to-many input data nodes, and these data's consumer lists contain this layer. A layer node can have one-to-many output data nodes, and these data's producer is this layer, which means that a data's consumer is a list and producer can have only one, from user direct input or from other layers. These identifiers of information are used for data layout and back-ends instruction generation processing stages.

The computational graph is built in high-level NN frameworks' kernel or operator functions such as Tensorflow or MXNet. And after several intermediate optimization steps, the graph backend calls NN accelerator compiler library APIs to generate binary NN instructions, which part is not being discussed in this work.

2.2 Intra Layer Loop Unrolling and Pipelining

At present, there are lots of scenarios for deep learning applications. The structure of the neural network model is usually formed during the training process, and the scale and parameters of NN layers are saved in model. When compile a neural network for accelerators, some of the values during optimization or existing in instruction fields can be replaced by constant value or immediate numbers. For example, the application scenario of convolutional neural network (CNN) in image recognition field is usually started with an input image. The image size can be fixed or dynamic. For a dynamic image size, we need a preprocess transformation (resize, crop, etc.) by which the image has been adjusted to the fixed scale as the network defined. And then do the forward inference.

In this situation, the condition branch judgment and the number of loops of the NN instructions are known ahead of time, which can reduce the programming jump and useless code to some extent. Therefore, we can implement a loop unrolling and pipelining to set loops with immediate numbers instead of through register scalar calculation.

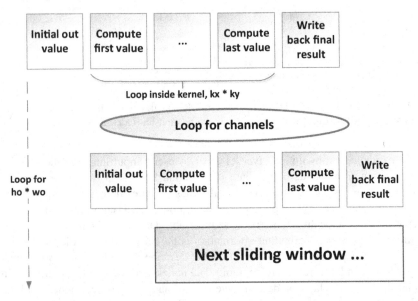

Fig. 2. A fine-grained pipelining example of a pooling layer. Unrolling static immediate number of loops for sliding windows with strides on channel, height and width dimension, and calculation using hardware corresponding units to get final results.

For more details, we consider the NN instructions of same type have the sequential assurance that different types of instructions can execute at the same time. Thus, we can use a ping-pong strategy of on-chip resource usage to parallel the stage of memory access and the stage of computation. The data fetching stage can be paralleled with calculation and write-back stage as shown in Fig. 2. In addition, data tiling can also be implemented with a naive static memory allocation, and divide the tensors into several tiling data slices in a layer's computing.

In some NN accelerators, a whole kernel's computation can be completed through one single NN instruction while the data fetching and scheduling are executed by hardware functional units simultaneously. Thus, we propose a higher level of parallel pipelining.

Since the calculation of neural network is mostly concentrated in convolution layers and fully-connected layer, in order to accelerate the calculation of neural network, the accelerators mostly use parallel multipliers and adders to carry out data parallel computation. In order to feed data in time to the accelerators function units, make a better use of data locality and enhance data reuse, some accelerators adopt on-chip-memory storage access hierarchy [12, 17, 18]. The NN layer computation process can be abstracted as follows: firstly, *load* necessary data slices into on-chip memory, then *calculation* is performed with the corresponding on-chip function units, and finally *store* the result slices to off-chip memory to complete the whole process of the NN layer operations.

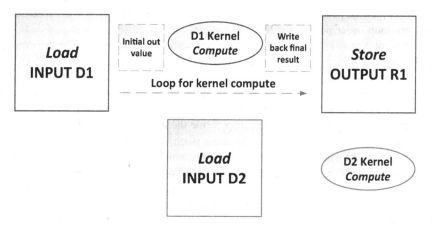

Fig. 3. A coarse-grained pipelining example of a pooling layer. D1 and D2 data allocate at symmetric on-chip memory address with ping-pong pipelining strategy. The static memory allocation method uses the shapes and parameters determined at compile time to adjust size of each data tiling slices. *Load* input slices with tiling size and on-chip memory allocation is at the beginning. And *computation* is paralleled with the load and store stage part of the opposite ping-pong memory data. *Store* output slices to off-chip memory and release the on-chip memory space at the end.

If we balance the execution time of the whole pipelining stage, which means the calculation functional units and IO units of the specific hardware back-end can work respectively at comparative time cost, we can cover the latency to some extent by using a type of coarse-grained pipelining (see Fig. 3). The period between synchronization instructions is called one time slice. During one time slice, previous store part of pipelining stage will execute at first so that can release corresponding on-chip memory space for next load pipelining stage to allocate and use for next input data slices. While the other half of resources are executing different type of instructions. Then the IO and computing functional units are working in parallel during one time slice, and so on. And data dependency between layers is solved through computation graph.

The coarse-grained pipelining focuses on on-chip memory computing access and interaction with off-chip memory. While fine-grained pipelining focuses on the instruction level parallel that inside the kernel calculation part. They both provide a novel programming pattern for NN accelerators. Using static memory allocation with ping-pong strategy, divide on-chip resources by half and re-arrange instructions to time slices to cover time cost. We call it stage level parallel. While programming on accelerators with on-chip memory and conflict-free functional units, in this pattern, we can deploy stage level parallel NN instructions without considering scheduling between layers. And development of operators can be modular.

2.3 Layer Fusion

In some deep learning frameworks or NN compiler frameworks [27, 31, 34], several types of layer fusion optimization has been implemented already. According to the stage level parallel programming style, we propose a layer fusion method based on its algorithm loop order pattern for NN accelerators.

In convolutional neural networks, there are some fixed patterns of layers combination, such as Convolution + Batch Normalization (BN) + Scale (SC) + Rectified Linear Unit (ReLU) layer, or Convolution + ReLU (or other activation layers), etc. However, these layers which follow the convolution layer, their memory cost functions are regular as well as their algorithms. For example, the BN layer and SC layer compute respectively for each feature map, while the ReLU layer is calculated on each independent number. The memory allocation is obviously to show that BN and SC layer both need extra memory space for constants which size is related to the number of feature map dimension or channel dimension. And all of them need one same size of memory space for input and output, or two equal spaces if on-chip memory cannot be reused during computation. Besides, from the algorithm view, all these layers do not have extra data dependence. In addition, their control flow of the computation is not complex. Therefore, a type of layer fusion optimization can be easily implemented as pipelining stages (see Fig. 4).

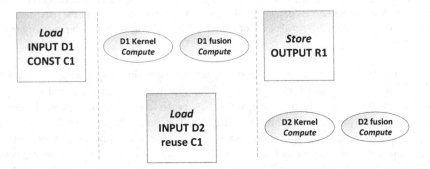

Fig. 4. An example of pipelining stage with fused layers. *Load* data blocks also contain necessary constant data for the fused layers. Next computing stages will reuse it until this constant data need to load next tiling slice. The allocation part in load pipelining stage in main layer also contain fused layers' memory cost function.

We call them the kernel-based computing layers, like convolution or pooling layer, as the main layer, and the latter layers that split their computing pipelining stage into the main layer's as the fused layers. And the layer fusion optimization also needs some information from the computational graph we mentioned in Sect. 2.1. One of the fusion optimization principles is that fused layers must have only one consumer and the data types of tensors between them must be compatible. And other rules are like based on a whitelist for the types of fused layers and fine-tuning for special specific performance. Another naive rule can be greedy strategy that if the next layer can be fused, we do the fusion optimization till no longer satisfy the constraints.

2.4   Layer Elimination

Several types of operations of frameworks have similar functions that to change data's order or expression of a tensor, such as reshape, transpose, squeeze, un-squeeze. If we regard the tensors as a long one-dimension data arrangement on memory space, in some situations these operations are redundant. In these situations, we do such layer elimination optimization.

We merge this layer's output and input data node, and so the consumer list. And then erase the layer node and its relationship, using the input data's producer to replace this layer for other data's producer. If the output and input have different memory spaces (such as in debug mode, need to be dumped), this layer can be replaced by a simple copy layer.

In this part, we should note that the original data order has effect on actual data layout in reshape layer. In frameworks a reshape layer's parameter is parsed in original data order to do reshape. While using NN accelerators as the computation back-end, the data could be needed to be re-tiled or re-formed as the specific shape or order to adapt the hardware compute patterns and scalable networks [16]. Due to the default data order is different in various frameworks, such as NCHW or NHWC, original data might be transposed or reshaped before the hardware really do the calculation. The intermediate data order could have changed. So, we need to restore the original data order and then reshape it, using a transpose layer and a reshape layer.

Besides remove or replace reshape-like layer nodes, transpose-like layers can also do optimization. After expand layers pipelining stages, if a sequence of layers only contains load and store stages to transpose data, we can merge them into one transpose layer. Naturally another principle is no other data dependencies upon these layers. So, there is no need for considering intermediate data nodes' consumer or producer relationship links.

3   Experiment Evaluation

In this section, we use Cambricon-Accelerator [16] as the prototype. The accelerator architecture has 32 leaf tiles as matrix function units. Each leaf tile has 24 KB SRAM, 32 16-bit adders and 32 16-bit multipliers. The central tile has 64 KB SRAM, 32 16-bit adders and 32 16-bit multipliers and transcendental function operators. The bank width of scratchpad memory is 512-bits (32 * 16-bit fixed point). The experiment result is based on a software simulator. And extra data type conversion and specific tiling of weight data in preprocess are not considered. We use Caffe deep learning framework for the test.

We choose several neural networks in image recognition field, GoogLeNet [22], VGG-16 [21], ResNet-50 [2] and MobileNet [25] and SqueezeNet [26] as a benchmark to evaluate the effect of layer fusion optimization. Database is on the ImageNet database [32]. And choose SSD [4] network in image detection field to evaluate layer elimination optimization. The chosen Database is on PASCAL VOC 2012 which test 1,000 images for average result.

The experiments results are showing as below (Figs. 5 and 6).

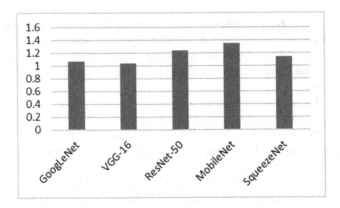

Fig. 5. Speedup ratio of open and close layer fusion optimization.

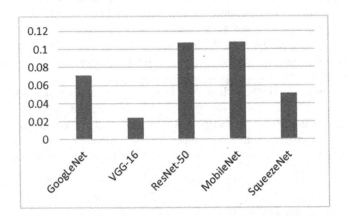

Fig. 6. NN instructions reduction ratio of with and without layer fusion optimization.

Amount of instructions is counted by NN instructions generator which we call it as the backend as the computational graph. From testing results we can find out that ResNet-50 and MobileNet have an obvious performance speedup because they have more easily-to-fuse structure in model. And GoogLeNet and VGG-16 speedup ratio is not so high might be their computation cost is occupied a large proportion in total time. Likely the SqueezeNet is more lightweight and structure is moderate for fusion optimization so its ratio is neither too large nor small in chart (Fig. 7).

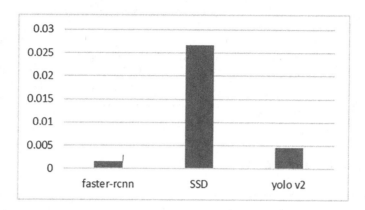

Fig. 7. Layer elimination optimization speedup ratio chart.

We choose VGG-16 as front-end network, and due to reshape-like layers exist a lot in SSD model, we can get a fair optimization effect, about 2.6% performance improvement on this model. The effect on the other two networks are not so obvious, less than 0.5%.

4 Related Work

There are already researches of neural networks from different levels of view in software, from top to bottom. Truong et al. designed Latte [33], a DNNs language that provides an abstraction for specifying new layers and a matched compiler based on user specification. It also applies general optimization and can generate instructions for heterogeneous architectures. However, in this work, a loop unrolling and pipelining is proposed from a higher level of abstraction. The optimization focuses on a stage level parallel (SLP) not the instruction level parallel (ILP).

There is yet another compiler framework for deep learning. T. Chen et al. proposed TVM [34] that can cope with workload across diversiform hardware back-ends. And apply graph-level and operator-level optimizations and also implement a type of layer fusion optimization to reduce memory access. While the fused layers must be injective reduction with complex-out-fusable layer such as convolution layer. SLP exposes the structure of coarse-grained pipelining stages, and offers the possibility to fuse complex-out-fusable layers.

Moreover Halide [35] is implemented as a low-level IR in TVM. Halide is a domain specific language in image processing field. It is designed to facilitate developers to write high-performance code with images and arrays across multiple operating systems. In general, it focuses on how data tiling and the order of value calculation and also data dependencies. While we use a static memory allocation and divide data for tiling by device on-chip memory size. Similarly, we are not in the same logic level.

While Intel proposed nGraph [36], an open source C++ library that simplifies the implementation of deep learning performance optimization across frameworks and hardware platforms. It is described as "framework-neutral software" and designated as the back-end of the framework. Input data can be obtained from popular machine learning frameworks such as TensorFlow, MXNet, PyTorch and CNTK. Its IR can deal with abstract details of hardware devices and make specific optimizations for different types of hardware backends, including CPUs. From this we are at the same level of NN software call stack. However, we concentrate on NN accelerators back-ends and nGraph are applying to handle CPUs and GPU mixed back-ends for better performance.

5 Conclusion and Future Work

Within the deep learning frameworks, users set up layers and parse the parameters through APIs to build the computational graph. With this information, we propose graph optimizations including layer elimination and layer fusion detection. According to the static scale and parameters of NN models, we use a static allocation for on-chip memory and do such loop unrolling and pipelining. By using a coarse-grained pipelining of a layer's computation, we abstract the NN algorithm operation into stages, called stage level parallel (SLP). With the SLP programming style, layer fusion optimization can be conveniently applied to fuse computation pipelining stages and reduce IO operations between layers, as well as memory allocation for intermediate tensor on off-chip memory. Our compilation optimizations for NN accelerator can be deployed for forward inference process.

However, there are still some aspects need to research in future work, such as training or fine-tuning of neural network is not completely involved yet. And certainly, as the updating of NN algorithms, more types of neural network layers can be developed in the programming style of pipelining stages.

Acknowledgement. This work is partially supported by the National Key Research and Development Program of China (under Grant 2017YFB1003104), the NSF of China (under Grants 61432016, 61532016, 61672491, 61602441, 61602446, 61732002, 61702478, 61732007 and 61732020), Beijing Natural Science Foundation (JQ18013), the 973 Program of China (under Grant 2015CB358800), National Science and Technology Major Project (2018ZX01 031102), the Transformation and Transfer of Scientific and Technological Achievements of Chinese Academy of Sciences (KFJ-HGZX-013), Key Research Projects in Frontier Science of Chinese Academy of Sciences (QYZDB-SSW-JSC001), Strategic Priority Research Program of Chinese Academy of Science (XDB32050200, XDC01020000) and Standardization Research Project of Chinese Academy of Sciences (BZ201800001).

References

1. Krizhevsky, A., Sutskever, I., Hinton, G.E.: ImageNet classification with deep convolutional neural networks. In: International Conference on Neural Information Processing Systems, pp. 1097–1105. Curran Associates Inc. (2012)
2. He, K., Zhang, X., Ren, S., et al.: Deep residual learning for image recognition, pp. 770–778 (2015)
3. Zhang, X., Zhou, X., Lin, M., et al.: ShuffleNet: an extremely efficient convolutional neural network for mobile devices (2017)
4. Liu, W., et al.: SSD: single shot MultiBox detector. In: Leibe, B., Matas, J., Sebe, N., Welling, M. (eds.) ECCV 2016. LNCS, vol. 9905, pp. 21–37. Springer, Cham (2016). https://doi.org/10.1007/978-3-319-46448-0_2
5. Ren, S., He, K., Girshick, R., et al.: Faster R-CNN: towards real-time object detection with region proposal networks. In: International Conference on Neural Information Processing Systems, pp. 91–99. MIT Press (2015)
6. Sak, H., Senior, A., Beaufays, F.: Long short-term memory recurrent neural network architectures for large scale acoustic modeling. Comput. Sci. 338–342 (2014)
7. Graves, A., Jaitly, N., Mohamed, A.R.: Hybrid speech recognition with deep bidirectional LSTM. In: Automatic Speech Recognition and Understanding, pp. 273–278. IEEE (2014)
8. Silver, D., Schrittwieser, J., Simonyan, K., et al.: Mastering the game of Go without human knowledge. Nature 550(7676), 354–359 (2017)
9. Silver, D., Huang, A., Maddison, C.J., et al.: Mastering the game of Go with deep neural networks and tree search. Nature 529(7587), 484–489 (2016)
10. OpenAI Five Homepage. https://blog.openai.com/openai-five/
11. Venkatesh, G., Nurvitadhi, E., Marr, D.: Accelerating deep convolutional networks using low-precision and sparsity (2016)
12. Ovtcharov, K., Ruwase, O., Kim, J., et al.: Accelerating deep convolutional neural networks using specialized hardware. Miscellaneous (2015)
13. Han, S., Liu, X., Mao, H., et al.: EIE: efficient inference engine on compressed deep neural network. In: International Symposium on Computer Architecture, pp. 243–254. IEEE Press (2016)
14. Zhang, C., Li, P., Sun, G., et al.: Optimizing FPGA-based accelerator design for deep convolutional neural networks. In: ACM/SIGDA International Symposium on Field-Programmable Gate Arrays, pp. 161–170. ACM (2015)
15. Parashar, A., Rhu, M., Mukkara, A., et al.: SCNN: an accelerator for compressed-sparse convolutional neural networks, pp. 27–40 (2017)
16. Chen, T., Du, Z., Sun, N.: DianNao: a small-footprint high-throughput accelerator for ubiquitous machine-learning. ACM SIGPLAN Not. 49(4), 269–284 (2014)
17. Chen, Y., Chen, T., Xu, Z.: DianNao family: energy-efficient hardware accelerators for machine learning. Commun. ACM 59(11), 105–112 (2016)
18. Zhang, S., Du, Z., Zhang, L., et al.: Cambricon-X: an accelerator for sparse neural networks. In: 2016 49th Annual IEEE/ACM International Symposium on Microarchitecture (MICRO). IEEE Computer Society (2016)
19. Liu, S., Du, Z., Tao, J., et al.: Cambricon: an instruction set architecture for neural networks. In: ACM/IEEE International Symposium on Computer Architecture, pp. 393–405. IEEE (2016)
20. Lecun, Y., Bottou, L., Bengio, Y., Haffner, P.: Gradient-based learning applied to document recognition. Proc. IEEE 86, 2278–2324 (1998)

21. Simonyan, K., Zisserman, A.: Very deep convolutional networks for large-scale image recognition. Comput. Sci. (2014)
22. Szegedy, C., Liu, W., Jia, Y., et al.: Going deeper with convolutions (2014)
23. Szegedy, C., Ioffe, S., Vanhoucke, V., et al.: Inception-v4, Inception-ResNet and the impact of residual connections on learning (2016)
24. Yu, F., Koltun, V.: Multi-scale context aggregation by dilated convolutions (2015)
25. Howard, A.G., Zhu, M., Chen, B., et al.: MobileNets: efficient convolutional neural networks for mobile vision applications (2017)
26. Iandola, F.N., Han, S., Moskewicz, M.W., et al.: SqueezeNet: AlexNet-level accuracy with 50x fewer parameters and <0.5 MB model size (2016)
27. Abadi, M., Agarwal, A., Barham, P., et al.: TensorFlow: large-scale machine learning on heterogeneous distributed systems (2016)
28. Jia, Y., Shelhamer, E., et al.: Caffe: convolutional architecture for fast feature embedding, pp. 675–678 (2014)
29. Chen, T., Li, M., Li, Y., et al.: MXNet: a flexible and efficient machine learning library for heterogeneous distributed systems. Statistics (2015)
30. Allan, V.H., Jones, R.B., Lee, R.M., et al.: Software pipelining. ACM Comput. Surv. **27**(3), 367–432 (1995)
31. Gray, A., Gottbrath, C., Olson, R., Prasanna, S., et al.: Production deep learning with NVIDIA GPU inference engine. https://devblogs.nvidia.com/production-deep-learning-nvidia-gpu-inference-engine/
32. Russakovsky, O., et al.: ImageNet large scale visual recognition challenge. Int. J. Comput. Vis. **115**(3), 211–252 (2015)
33. Truong, L., Barik, R., Totoni, E., et al.: Latte: a language, compiler, and runtime for elegant and efficient deep neural networks. In: ACM SIGPLAN Conference on Programming Language Design and Implementation, pp. 209–223. ACM (2016)
34. Chen, T., Moreau, T., Jiang, Z., et al.: TVM: an automated end-to-end optimizing compiler for deep learning (2018)
35. Ragankelley, J., Adams, A., Sharlet, D., et al.: Halide: decoupling algorithms from schedules for high-performance image processing. Commun. ACM **61**(1), 106–115 (2018)
36. Cyphers, S., Bansal, A.K., Bhiwandiwalla, A., et al.: Intel nGraph: an intermediate representation, compiler, and executor for deep learning (2018)

ZhuQue: A Neural Network Programming Model Based on Labeled Data Layout

Weijian Du[1,2,3(✉)], Linyang Wu[1,2,3], Xiaobing Chen[1,2,3],
Yimin Zhuang[1,2,3], and Tian Zhi[1,3]

[1] SKL of Computer Architecture, Institute of Computing Technology, CAS,
Beijing, China
{duweijian,wulinyang,chenxiaobing,zhuangyimin,
zhitian}@ict.ac.cn
[2] University of Chinese Academy of Sciences, Beijing, China
[3] Cambricon Tech. Ltd., Shanghai, China

Abstract. In the last five years, the research of neural network accelerators has made remarkable achievements and provided powerful hardware support for many deep learning algorithms. In order to improve the performance of the neural network accelerator, algorithm optimization and data layout in the neural network development kit (NDK) are indispensable. The rich data types in neural network algorithms determine the diversity of data layout information. How to add complex data layout information to the NDK, to guide the work of all aspects of the software, to avoid user perception and to provide a user-friendly API, has become a series of issues worth studying. This paper implements a neural network development kit based on labeled data layout to solve the above problems, and abstracts a neural network programming model. The programming model establishes a neural network computing graph at "creating time", "compiling time" sets the data label and "runtime" uses the label to control the data transfer. Compared with the existing NDK, the software has an average performance improvement of 4.76×. In addition, this paper also defines dynamic tags and static tags of neural network data, and proposes a neural network data classification method.

Keywords: Neural network · Programming model · Labeled · Data layout · SDK

1 Introduction

Background. In recent years, the research of AI (Artificial Intelligence) has made remarkable achievements. Good algorithms and ideas have appeared in the field of image recognition, object detection, natural language processing and so on. Practice has proved that deep learning is still the best technology for the above applications. However, deep learning algorithms are computing intensive and memory intensive. The traditional way of relying on CPU server cluster has low speed and high power, which is obviously unacceptable. Therefore, many research work has turned to GPU,

© Springer Nature Switzerland AG 2019
P.-C. Yew et al. (Eds.): APPT 2019, LNCS 11719, pp. 27–39, 2019.
https://doi.org/10.1007/978-3-030-29611-7_3

FPGA and neural network ASIC (such as TPU, DianNao [8], etc.), hoping to use this hardware to accelerate AI applications.

Meanwhile, in order to facilitate users to use hardware products, chip design companies launch corresponding software development tools to shield hardware details and provide high-level interface. For example, cuDNN for NVIDIA GPU, MIOpen for AMD GPU, CNML [12] for Cambricon MLU and so on. These SDKs usually enable the neural network operations to achieve high performance on their corresponding hardware. We call them NDK (Neural network Development Kit).

Motivation. In order to give hardware full performance, it is essential to optimize the neural network algorithm and data layout. A feasible solution is to add algorithm optimization and data layout to NDK. Because this can not only shield hardware details, so that users do not have to pay too much attention to hardware, but also facilitate the full use of hardware resources, so that the hardware can get high performance. But there are two problems that need to be solved. Firstly, how to add data layout information in NDK, and this information can run through all modules of NDK. Secondly, how to avoid users' perception of data layout information and facilitate user programming.

Our Work. In this paper, we propose ZhuQue, a neural network programming model based on labeled data layout, to solve the above two problems. Firstly, we study the data classification method of neural network (NNDataClass) and what content should be included in the label. By analyzing the memory bandwidth requirement of data access, the location of data in the network, the reading and writing behavior of data, we classify the neural network data into eight classes, and the characteristics of different types of data are different. This classification is also applicable to CPU, GPU, NN accelerator and other hardware platforms.

Then, we design and implement a neural network development kit with labeled data layout(LDL-NDK) for Cambricon-X [13] hardware platform and abstract the ZhuQue programming model. The development kit implements three levels of functions. The first level "creating time" provides computing graph components for users to describe neural network computing graphs. The second level "compiling time" realizes the functions of label setting and instruction generating, and is the main module of hardware performance optimization. The third level "runtime" implements labeled memory operation and graph computing. The label of the data layout is set at compiling time and used at runtime.

Finally, we choose two experimental platforms, Cambricon-X with DLPlib [14] and Cambricon-X with ZhuQue, to test the computing time of several single-layer networks and multi-layer networks. The average computing time of ZhuQue-Cambricon-X is $4.76\times$ faster than DLPlib-Cambricon-X.

Contributions. The contributions of this paper are as follows.

- We propose a data classification standard for neural networks (NNDataClass). It is convenient for NDK to optimize the layout of different types of data and improve hardware performance.

- We implement a neural network development kit with labeled data layout (LDL-NDK). This tool is designed for Cambricon-X hardware platform, and achieves an average performance improvement of 4.76× faster than DLPlib-Cambricon-X.
- We abstract a neural network programming model (ZhuQue). It can not only avoid users' perception of data layout information and facilitate user programming, but also enable data layout information to be transmitted in NDK.

The rest of this paper is organized as follows. Section 2 shows the related work of neural network accelerator, data layout and labeled architecture. Section 3 introduces the content of label and the data classification standard of neural network (NNData-Class). Section 4 introduces the design and implementation of LDL-NDK. Section 5 abstracts the ZhuQue programming model. Section 6 is a series of experiments. Section 7 makes the conclusion of this paper.

2 Related Work

Neural Network Accelerator. Through observing the research and commercial application in the last five years, it can be found that the hardware computing carriers of the neural network algorithm mainly include CPU, GPU, FPGA and ASIC. CPU and GPU, as general processors, have the widest application fields and support the most neural network operations. Almost all of the neural network framework software supports CPU and GPU computing, such as Caffe [15], TensorFlow [9], MXNet [10] and so on. Because of the particularity of neural network algorithm, its special processor can get faster speed, lower power, smaller chip area and lower cost. For example, Farabet et al. [7] implemented a real-time face detection convolutional network on a single FPGA, which can be used for low-power vision systems. Of course, the most famous neural network accelerator is the DianNao series [1, 5, 6, 8, 13]. Its latest Cambricon-X [13] supports both dense and sparse neural networks and is 7.23× faster than DianNao. Cambricon-X is chosen as the hardware platform for our later experiments.

Data Layout. One of the classical methods in data layout is DAT (data alignment technology) method proposed by Panda et al. [2], which improves cache hit rate by complement, data alignment and cyclic fragmentation of matrix. However, this method requires software developers to optimize themselves, and need to understand the cache structure and parameters. If a machine is replaced, the optimization scheme needs to be readjusted. Coleman et al. [3] proposed an algorithm for calculating the size of matrix fragments. The algorithm points out how to choose the size of fragments according to the size of cache and matrix. This method gives a formula solving method, which makes matrix multiplication fragments quantifiable, and it is a great progress. Liu et al. [4] proposed a data conversion system DL, which can realize the conversion of data layout in heterogeneous computing scenarios of CPU and GPU. For the two processors, the hit rate of each cache can be improved.

Labeled Architecture. Labeled Von Neumann Architecture is proposed by Huang et al. [11]. They believe that the separation of storage and computation in traditional

Von Neumann Architecture leads to memory wall problems. Multilevel cache can solve this problem, but when cache is shared by multiple cores (such as L3cache), new problems of inter-core competition will arise. So they set label to data, pass it from software to hardware, and let the hardware decide the replacement of data in cache according to the priority recorded on the label. This reduces the competition for shared cache and improves CPU utilization. However, this method needs to be modified from bottom to top, from hardware to software, which is more difficult to popularize and apply, because it is not easy to accept the time and cost for users to reconstruct existing computers and even replace CPU and memory in large quantities. This enlightens us that labeled transformation should be done at the software level as far as possible.

3 Data Label

In order to add labels for data layout in NDK, we need to define the content of labels first. We divide label into static label and dynamic label. Static label refer to hardware-independent information, which is related to neural network algorithms and data node location in the computing graph. Dynamic label is hardware-related information, which is mainly used to lay out data as the best state on specific hardware.

3.1 Static Label

First, we analyze the bandwidth requirement of neural network data. Let's take a single-batch MLP operation as an example. We can find that the calculation of MLP involves four pieces of data: input neurons, weights, bias and output neurons. If the number of input neurons is equal to output neurons (in.size() = out.size() = n), then the memory access of bias, input and output neurons is n, but the weights is n^2. Therefore, we can divide the neural network data into two categories: neurons and weights. Convolution also contains neurons and weights, but pooling and LRN have only neurons.

Secondly, we analyze the location of data in the neural network topology. Figure 1 is an example of a simple neural network, which consists of two layers, MLP and active. We can subdivide the aforementioned neurons into input neurons, hidden neurons and output neurons. Similarly, weights can be subdivided into input weights and output weights. Output weights are usually used for training networks, while input weights are used for inference networks and training networks.

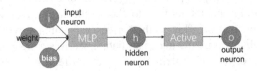

Fig. 1. An example of two-layer neural network.

Thirdly, we analyze the reading and writing behavior of data. After training, the weights and bias of MLP are fixed, so they will not change during inference. If a inference network is executed many times and using different input data each time, the user only needs to write the weight and bias once, while the input neuron needs to write many times. In this case, the data can be divided into constants and variables. Therefore, we obtain two new classes, constant neurons and constant weights.

In addition, the hardware instruction is indispensable for the calculation of the neural network, so the instruction is also a kind of data. This kind of data does not participate in the calculation, but controls the calculation.

So far, we summarize the characteristics of eight types of data as shown in Table 1, which can be used as a classification standard of neural network data. We call it NNDataClass. Because this classification method has nothing to do with hardware, it can be used as a static label of neural network data.

Table 1. NNDataClass: the classification standard of neural network data.

Static label	Data classification	Bandwidth requirement	Location in network	Inst read/write	User read/write	Participate or control calculation
Inst	Instruction	low	NA	read only	invisible	C
IN	Input Neuron	low	input	read only	write	P
ON	Output Neuron	low	output	r/w	read	P
HN	Hidden Neuron	low	middle	r/w	not care	P
CN	Constant Neuron	low	input	read only	write once	P
IW	Input Weight	high	input	read only	write	P
OW	Output Weight	high	output	r/w	read	P
CW	Constant Weight	high	input	read only	write once	P

3.2 Dynamic Label

Dynamic label contains hardware-related information, which is mainly used to lay out data as the best state on specific hardware. Assuming that there is a hardware including vector inner product unit, it can calculate eight float16 data at a time. If there are more than eight numbers, it needs to be calculated in batches. If there are less than eight numbers, it needs to be filled up to eight numbers. Suppose that in the example of MLP in Sect. 3.1, input neuron vector has 10 float32 data, weight matrix has 10 * 4 float32 data. In this example, we can optimize the accuracy, matrix transposition, tiling and padding of data.

Firstly, in order to make the hardware work, it is necessary to convert float32 data to float16. Secondly, in order to improve memory access efficiency, the weight matrix can be transferred from row-first storage to column-first storage. Thirdly, in order to adapt to the limitation of vector inner product unit, it is necessary to divide the input neuron and weight matrix into 8 + 2 two pieces. Fourthly, in order to make full use of the hardware performance, the second piece of data can be filled up by 6 zeros, which is just 8 numbers. Figure 2 shows these four steps.

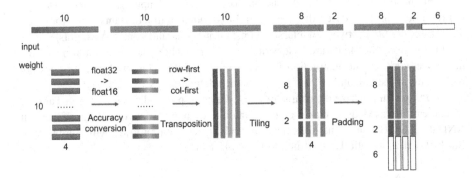

Fig. 2. Four steps of data layout optimization to input neuron and weight.

In the above data layout optimization process, at least the following information is needed: data accuracy, row-first storage or column-first storage, tiling size, padding size. These can be used as dynamic labels for this specific hardware.

To sum up, we can set labels for input neurons of MLP is (IN; accuracy = float32->float16, storage = row, tiling = 8, padding = 6), and labels for weight is (IW; accuracy = float32->float16, storage = row->col, tiling = 8, padding = 6). This is the label used in data layout, including static label and dynamic label.

4   LDL-NDK

In this section, we introduce the design and implement of neural network development kit with labeled data layout (LDL-NDK) based on Cambricon-X hardware platform. We design the LDL-NDK as three levels.

The first level "creating time" implements three components: data node, operation node and computing graph. Users could describe neural network computing graphs by these data structure.

The second level "compiling time" provides compiling function, which can compile the network topology from the previous level. It contains computing graph scanner and instruction generator. Data layout label is set in this level. Computing graph scanner set static label and instruction generator set dynamic label.

The third level "runtime" contains three components: device management unit, memory management unit and data layout executor. It mainly provides two kinds of functions: labeled memory operation and graph computing. The label of the data layout is used at these two functions. A simple software architecture is shown in Fig. 3.

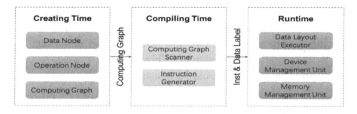

Fig. 3. LDL-NDK software architecture.

4.1   Creating Time

Data Node. Data nodes record attributes (or labels) of data and link relationships with operation nodes. Some static labels require users to set them in constructors, such as the accuracy of data, the order of dimensions and the size of each dimension. The other part of static labels and all dynamic labels are automatically set by the software at the later compiling time. For example, a 10 * 4, float32, row-first matrix should be constructed in this way:

```
DataNode_t weight;
createDataNode(weight, FLOAT32, DIM_HW, {10, 4});
```

Each data node can only link one producer operation node, that is, the degree of entry is 1, but it can link multiple consumer nodes, that is, the degree of output is not less than 1. Its visualization is shown in Fig. 4.

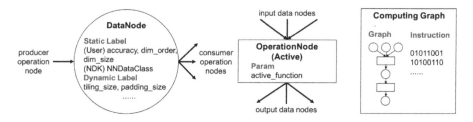

Fig. 4. Data node, operation node and computing graph structure.

Operation Node. Operation node is a general term. Each kind of neural network operation corresponds to an operation node. This is because different operation need to record different parameters, and the number of input and output data nodes connected by different operators is also different.

For example, convolution operations need to record the size of kernels, strides and pads. It has three input data nodes and one output data node. Activation operations need to record the type of activation function, which has an input data node and an output data node. Its visualization is shown in Fig. 4.

A ReLU activation operations should be constructed in this way:

```
DataNode_t in, out;
OperationNode_t act;
createActiveOp(act, in, out, ACT_FUNC_RELU);
```

In the constructor of the operation node, we establish the connection between the data node and the operation node, so that we have two elements of the graph: point and edge.

Computing Graph. Computing graph is a container that contains many data nodes, operation nodes and their connecting edges. Since the edge between the data node and the operation node has been established when the operation node is created, only the operation node can be recorded when the calculation graph is created. The two-layer neural network example in Fig. 1 could be constructed in this way:

```
DataNode_t i, w, b, h, o;
OperationNode_t mlp, act;
createMlpOp(mlp, i, w, b, h);
createActiveOp(act, h, o, ACT_FUNC_RELU);
CGraph_t cg;
createCGraph(cg, {mlp, act});
```

The instruction is also stored in computing graph. They will be generated in the compiling time. Its visualization is shown in Fig. 4.

4.2   Compiling Time

This level of LDL-NDK only provides a compiling function to users.

```
compileCGraph(cg);
```

But it contains two components that are invisible to users.

Computing Graph Scanner. According to the data structures in Sect. 4.1, we design a "double queue width first graph traversal" algorithm (DQWFGT) to scan the computing graph and set the static label (NNDataClass) of the data node.

Algorithm 1. Double queue width first graph traversal (DQWFGT)
1.   Initialize data node queue *dq* as all input data nodes of network;
2.   Initialize operation node queue *oq* as NULL;
3.   **while** (*dq* != NULL) **do**
4.   *oq.add*(all unmarked operation nodes in *dq.head().consumer()*)
5.   **while** (*op* has head node *hon*) **do**
6.   **for** each data node *idn* in *hon.inputNode()*
7.   *setNNDataClass(idn, hon, idn.inputdegree())*;
8.   **end**
9.   **for** each data node *odn* in *hon.outputNode()*
10.   *setNNDataClass(odn, hon, odn.outputdegree())*;
11.   **if** *odn.outputdegree() > 0*
12.   *dq.add(odn)*;
13.   **end**
14.   **end**
15.   mark and delete *hon* in *op*;
16.   **end**
17.   *dq.pophead()*;
18.   **end**

Instruction Generator. According to the characteristics of hardware, the instruction generator optimizes the algorithm of the computing graph, writes the information needed for data layout (such as tiling and padding) into the dynamic label of the data node, compiles and generates instructions. In addition, it also calculates the size of the space occupied by a data after layout optimization, which is convenient for later steps.

So far, all static and dynamic labels have been set up. In the example of Sect. 3.2, the complete label of weight looks like this: (static: IW, Float32, DIM_HW, {10, 4}; dynamic: Float16, DIM_WH, tiling = 8, padding = 6, size = 128Byte). And $128 = (10 + 6) * 4 * sizeof(Float16)$.

4.3   Runtime

Labeled Memory Operation. Traditional memory allocation functions only need to fill in the size of memory space, and then the operating system allocates such large memory space to users. Traditional memory copy function is to copy the data to another memory area intact. However, it is not enough for the neural network data with layout optimization, because the size of device memory required for data is no longer the original size, and the data copy between host memory and device memory also needs to go through data layout. Therefore, we add label control to memory allocation and memory copy functions in LDL-NDK. The data layout executor will lay out the data first according to the size and layout information in the label. Then the memory management unit finish memory allocation and memory copy. But user API is simple, just like this:

```
DataNode_t weight
void* wp;
labelMalloc(&wp, weight);
labelMemcpy(wp, wp_cpu, weight, HostToDevice);
```

Graph Computing. This function first uses the memory management unit to copy the instructions saved in the computing graph into the device memory, and then starts the hardware calculation under the control of the device management unit. But user API is very simple, just like this:

```
computeCGraph(cg);
```

5   ZhuQue Programming Model

The ZhuQue programming model is abstracted from LDL-NDK. There are three steps when using it, just like Fig. 5.

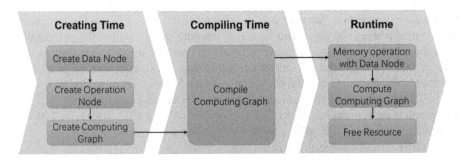

Fig. 5. ZhuQue programming model main steps.

Users create data nodes, operation nodes and computing graph in Creating Time according to the topological structure of neural network. Users also need to set some static labels when creating data nodes, such as the accuracy of data, the order of dimensions and the size of each dimension.

Users call an API at Compiling Time to optimize the algorithm and generate hardware instructions. This API function sets static labels and dynamic labels for data nodes.

At runtime, users need to use data nodes to apply for space in device memory and copy data to device memory, then call a function to finish computing, finally release resources.

This programming model can not only avoid users' perception of data layout information and facilitate user programming, but also enable data layout information to be transmitted in NDK.

6 Experiment

Hardware Platform. We implemented a Cambricon-X simulator with Verilog. The architecture consists of 16 PEs (processing elements). Each PE contains 16 multipliers and an adder tree, which can calculate the vector inner product of 16 half-precision floating-point numbers. The SB (synapse buffer) of each PE has 2 KB. All PEs share an 8 KB NBin and an 8 KB NBout (neuron buffer). The frequency of the simulator can reach 1 GHz. We use VCS (Synopsys Verilog Compiler Simulator) to compile and simulate the architecture. The reasons why we choose Cambricon-X instead of GPU or CPU are as follows: 1. Cambricon-X is a representative neural network accelerator, its architecture is clearer and easier to implement than GPU and CPU; 2. GPU already has corresponding NDK, such as NVIDIA's cuDNN, we have little significance to do NDK for GPU; 3. The NDK of Cambricon-X has DLPlib, which is convenient for us to do comparative experiments. Of course, the method of labeled data layout can also be migrated to the NDK of GPU and CPU.

Benchmark. We choose 10 test cases, including 2 multi-layer neural networks and 8 single-layer neural networks. Multi-layer neural networks consist of two typical image classification networks, AlexNet and VGG16. The single-layer neural networks include four common operations, convolution, pooling, MLP and matrix multiplication. Their parameters and data scale are shown in Table 2.

Table 2. Single-layer benchmarks.

Operation	Input (h * w * c)	Output (h * w * c)	Kernel (h * w)	Stride (h, w)	Pad (h, w)
Conv1	112 * 112 * 96	112 * 112 * 384	3 * 3	1, 1	1, 1
Conv2	112 * 112 * 96	112 * 112 * 256	3 * 3	1, 1	1, 1
Pool1	55 * 55 * 96	27 * 27 * 96	3 * 3	2, 2	0, 0
Pool2	224 * 224 * 64	112 * 112 * 64	2 * 2	2, 2	0, 0
MLP1	1 * 4096 * 1	1 * 4096 * 1	4096 * 4096	–	–
MLP2	1 * 4096 * 1	1 * 1000 * 1	4096 * 1000	–	–
MM1	256 * 256 * 1	256 * 256 * 1	256 * 256	–	–
MM2	512 * 512 * 1	512 * 512 * 1	512 * 512	–	–

Results. The above 10 test cases were implemented using ZhuQue and DLPlib, respectively, running on the Cambricon-X simulator. Each test case was run three times, taking the average of the calculated time. The test results are shown in Fig. 6.

We can find that the average speedup of single-layer neural network is 5.27× and that of multi-layer neural network is 2.72×. So the average speedup is 4.76×. For single-layer neural networks, the reason ZhuQue is faster than DLPlib is that ZhuQue joins the optimization of data layout. The instruction generator gives a good data layout scheme for the buffer size of Cambricon-X. The reason why multi-layer neural networks get faster is that ZhuQue has added labeled data layout on the one hand, and

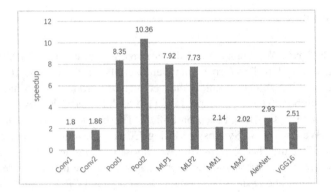

Fig. 6. The speedup of ZhuQue over DLPlib.

DLPlib has not done cross-layer optimization on the other hand. Cross-layer optimization means that the output result of the previous layer resides on the chip and is directly used for the calculation of the next layer. It does not need to be stored outside the chip and then read into the chip.

7 Conclusion

This paper defines the dynamic label and static label of neural network data, proposes a neural network data classification method NNDataClass, implements a neural network development kit LDL-NDK based on labeled data layout, and finally abstracts the neural network programming model ZhuQue based on labeled data layout, which achieves a performance improvement of 4.76× faster than the existing NDK. Our future work will focus on supporting more operations, exploring ways to further improve performance, and studying how to apply labeled data layout to multi-core neural network accelerators.

Acknowledgement. This work is partially supported by the National Key Research and Development Program of China (under Grant 2017YFB1003101), the NSF of China (under Grants 61432016, 61532016, 61672491, 61602441, 61602446, 61732002, 61702478, 61732007 and 61732020), Beijing Natural Science Foundation (JQ18013), the 973 Program of China (under Grant 2015CB358800), National Science and Technology Major Project (2018ZX01031102), the Transformation and Transfer of Scientific and Technological Achievements of Chinese Academy of Sciences (KFJ-HGZX-013), Key Research Projects in Frontier Science of Chinese Academy of Sciences (QYZDB-SSW-JSC001), Strategic Priority Research Program of Chinese Academy of Science (XDB32050200, XDC01020000) and Standardization Research Project of Chinese Academy of Sciences (BZ201800001).

References

1. Zidong, D., Robert, F., Tianshi, C., et al.: ShiDianNao: shifting vision processing closer to the sensor. In: Proceedings of the 42nd Annual International Symposium on Computer Architecture (ISCA), pp. 92–104. ACM (2015)
2. Panda, P.R., Nakamura, H., Dutt, N.D., Nicolau, A.: Augmenting loop tiling with data alignment for improved cache performance. IEEE Trans. Comput. **48**(2), 142–149 (1999)
3. Coleman, S., Mckinley, K.S.: Tile size selection using cache organization and data layout. ACM SIGPLAN Not. **30**(6), 279–290 (1995)
4. Liu, G.D., Hwu, W.W.: DL: a data layout transformation system for heterogeneous computing. In: Innovative Parallel Computing. IEEE (2012)
5. Yunji, C., Tao, L., Shaoli, L., et al.: DaDianNao: a machine-learning supercomputer. In: Proceedings of the 47th Annual IEEE/ACM International Symposium on Microarchitecture, MICRO-47, pp. 609–622 (2014)
6. Liu, D., Chen, T., Liu, S., et al.: PuDianNao: a polyvalent machine learning accelerator. In: Twentieth International Conference on Architectural Support for Programming Languages & Operating Systems (2015)
7. Clément, F., Cyril, P., Jefferson, Y.H., Yann, L.: CNP: an FPGA-based processor for convolutional networks. In: International Conference on Field Programmable Logic & Applications. IEEE (2009)
8. Tianshi, C., Zidong, D., Ninghui, S., et al.: DianNao: a small-footprint high-throughput accelerator for ubiquitous machine-learning. In: Proceedings of the 19th International Conference on Architectural Support for Programming Languages and Operating Systems (ASPLOS), pp. 269–284 (2014)
9. Abadi, M., Barham, P., Chen, J., et al.: TensorFlow: a system for large-scale machine learning. In: Operating Systems Design and Implementation, OSDI 2016, pp. 265–283 (2016)
10. Tianqi, C., Mu, L., Yutian, L., et al.: MXNet: a flexible and efficient machine learning library for heterogeneous distributed systems. Statistics (2015)
11. Huang, B., Yu, Z., Zhang, L., et al.: Supporting differentiated services in computers via programmable architecture for resourcing-on-demand (PARD). In: Twentieth International Conference on Architectural Support for Programming Languages & Operating Systems. ACM (2015)
12. CNML: Cambricon NeuWare Machine Learning Library. http://www.cambricon.com/index. php?c=page&id=21. Accessed 10 Apr 2019
13. Shijin, Z., Zidong, D., Lei, Z., et al.: Cambricon-X: an accelerator for sparse neural networks. In: Proceedings of the 49th Annual IEEE/ACM International Symposium on Microarchitecture. ACM (2016)
14. Hui-Ying, L., Lin-Yang, W., Xiao, Z., et al.: DLPlib: a library for deep learning processor. 计算机科学技术学报: 英文版 (2), 286–296 (2017)
15. Yangqing, J., Evan, S., Jeff, D., et al.: Caffe: convolutional architecture for fast feature embedding (2014)

Scheduling and File Systems

Reducing Rename Overhead
in Full-Path-Indexed File System

Longhua Wang[1,2], Youyou Lu[1,2], Siyang Li[1,2], Fan Yang[1,2], and Jiwu Shu[1,2(✉)]

[1] Department of Computer Science and Technology,
Tsinghua University, Beijing, China
{wanglh16,yangf17}@mails.tsinghua.edu.cn,
{luyouyou,lisiyang,shujw}@tsinghua.edu.cn
[2] Tsinghua National Laboratory for Information Science and Technology,
Beijing, China

Abstract. Full-path-indexed file systems use a key-value database to store the full path names of files and their metadata. With this pattern, the I/O efficiency can be improved because data is placed on persistent storage in scan order. However, it introduces intolerable overhead on renaming a directory because of the modification on the full path names of files under that directory. In this paper, we introduce *prefix replacement* mechanism on B+-tree to accelerate renaming directories on full-path-indexed file systems. It consists of three steps: *pre-scan prefix deletion, key replacement* and *floating-split bulk insertion*. Unnecessary searches and compares reduced in these mechanisms. We use Kyoto Cabinet as the key-value database, and implement *prefix replacement* mechanism on it. We run tests on two benchmarks, the first is generated by Mdtest [18], and the second is the source code of Linux [19]. Compared with LocoFS [4], one kind of full-path-indexed file system, our design is about 5× faster to rename large directories, and the performance is basically same on small directories.

Keywords: File system management · Full-path-indexed file system · Key-value store · B+-tree

1 Introduction

Full-path indexing is recently used on modern file systems to improve the performance of random write. Full-path-indexed file systems use full path name as indexing to store data and/or metadata. Files are placed in lexicographic order, so scans of any directory (e.g., ls -R or grep -r) can run at near disk bandwidth. Full-path-indexed file systems perform well on nearly all operations, and are becoming more and more prevalent in both stand-alone file systems [3,5–8] and distributed file systems [2,4,10,15,16,21,22]. However, they suffer from renaming directories [5–7]. The full path name of a file consists of two parts, the pathname and the filename. It changes the pathnames of all files under the

© Springer Nature Switzerland AG 2019
P.-C. Yew et al. (Eds.): APPT 2019, LNCS 11719, pp. 43–54, 2019.
https://doi.org/10.1007/978-3-030-29611-7_4

directory when renaming, so the full path names should be changed correspondingly. When renaming directories, it has a miserable performance to maintain full-path order for the whole file system, especially on large directories.

Most full-path-indexed file systems use key-value databases to store indexes. In order to look up metadata with one I/O request, some systems use hash table [23], which harms locality because files under the same directory may be scattered across the disk. Some file systems are built on Write-Optimized Dictionaries (or WODs), which include Log-Structured Merge Trees (LSM-trees) [11,13], B^ϵ-trees [14] and their variants. But to modify the full path names of files under a directory, it may cause thousands, even millions *get, remove* and *set* requests to database [4–7]. Some file systems even do not allow renaming directories [10].

Our Contributions. We propose an advanced B+-tree that supports *pre-scan prefix deletion, key replacement* and *floating-split bulk insertion* mechanisms which remove and insert a series of consecutive records efficiently. With these mechanisms, we further implement high-performance *prefix replacement*, which supports efficient renaming on full-path-indexed file systems. We propose *pre-scan prefix deletion, key replacement* and *floating-split bulk insertion* steps to avoid unnecessary compares and searches in database. Our proposed advanced B+-tree supports fast tree operations such as ① fast cutting out a sub-tree, ② fast inserting a sub-tree and ③ fast replacing records with a specific prefix. We use these operations to implement recursively removing, recursively copying and renaming directories, and compare the results with LocoFS. Our evaluations show that it is about ① 4× faster than LocoFS to remove directories recursively, ② 6× faster than LocoFS to copy directories recursively and ③ 5× faster than LocoFS to rename directories.

2   Motivation

Full-path indexing is widely used in file systems to improve directory locality. However, it changes the pathnames of all files under the directory to rename. It is not in an I/O-efficient manner and incurs prohibitively high overheads. For example, the whole system needs to be scanned when renaming is performed in hash-based key-value stores [17,23]. In tree-based key-value databases, it incurs substantial overheads to rename a directory because the records should be modified one by one [3–7,12]. The state-of-the-art solution [9] cuts out a sub-tree and pastes it to a proper position. However, it complicates the definition of B^ϵ-tree, making it hard to transplant.

LocoFS is a typical full-path indexing file system. It uses full-path indexing to store the metadata, and obtains good performance on *touch, mkdir, rmdir* and *rm* operations. However, it suffers from renaming directories. Taking renaming the directory /s to /z as an example, the procedures in LocoFS [4] are: ① initialize *cursor* at /s and get the record, ② check whether the record takes /s/ as a prefix (or whether the record is /s). If it does, ③ replace the prefix /s to /z, then set the modified record into the tree and ④ remove the old record,

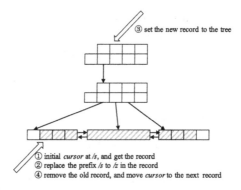

③ set the new record to the tree

① initial *cursor* at /s, and get the record
② replace the prefix /s to /z in the record
④ remove the old record, and move *cursor* to the next record

Fig. 1. Rename the directory /s to /z in LocoFS. The striped records should be replaced.

and move *cursor* to the next record. Figure 1 depicts this procedure, the target records are in stripe. Because the pathnames are same (under a directory), so the records will be continuously stored in the tree after insertion.

LocoFS removes and sets records one by one while renaming a directory. However, we observe that plenty of redundant searches and compares could be eliminated if these records are removed and inserted in bulk mode. In order to implement this idea, we propose *pre-scan prefix deletion*, *key replacement* and *floating-split bulk insertion* mechanisms.

3   Design and Implementation

3.1   Overview

We introduce a new efficient mechanism called *prefix replacement* on B+-tree. To rename directory /s to /z, *prefix replacement* replaces /s to /z, and changes the prefix /s to /z on all records that take /s/ as a prefix. So renaming a directory on full-path-indexed file systems could be transformed into one simple *prefix replacement* on the database. When a thread renaming a directory, it possesses an exclusive lock of the database to avoid consistency conflicts. *Prefix replacement* involves three steps:

- *Pre-scan prefix deletion* (in Sect. 3.2)
- *Key replacement* (in Sect. 3.3)
- *Floating-split bulk insertion* (in Sect. 3.4)

In *pre-scan prefix deletion*, we cut out the sub-tree whose records take /s/ as a prefix (and the record /s). The indexes and internal nodes in the sub-tree are released, while records and leaves in the sub-tree are saved. Then we replace the prefix from /s to /z in the records, which is called *key replacement*. In *floating-split bulk insertion*, we insert the modified leaves into the tree and construct indexes that point to them.

We use Kyoto Cabinet, an implementation of the key-value store, to implement and test *prefix replacement*. There is a difference in the definition of B+-tree in Kyoto Cabinet. A node is legal as long as it is not empty and not oversized. We utilize this characteristic to simplify *prefix replacement* and demonstrate how to generalize it (in Sect. 3.5).

3.2   Pre-scan Prefix Deletion

The goal of *pre-scan prefix deletion* is to cut out the sub-tree whose records take /*s*/ as a prefix (and the record /*s*). Figure 2 shows the procedure of *pre-scan prefix deletion*. We divide *pre-scan prefix deletion* into two steps. The first step is pre-scan (shown in Fig. 2(a) and (b)), which distinguishes the sub-tree that contains target records, and the second is cutting it out (shown in Fig. 2(b) and (c)). We release the memory of the internal nodes in the sub-tree, and maintain the memory of the leaves.

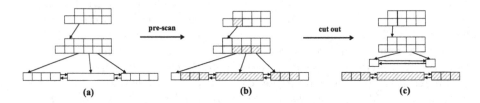

Fig. 2. *Pre-scan prefix deletion* procedure. We use pre-scan mechanism to distinguish the sub-tree (marked in stripe) that contains target records, then cut the sub-tree.

In order to locate the indexes that point to the sub-tree containing target records efficiently, we design a two-step binary search mechanism. Figure 3 introduces how two-step binary search works.

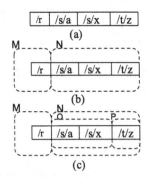

Fig. 3. Two-step binary search

In Fig. 3(a), we binary search /*s*/ in the node to find the smallest index that greater than /*s*/, and divide the indexes into two parts. Mark them as M and

N (shown in Fig. 3(b)), the indexes in N are greater than $/s/$, and indexes in M do not. The indexes that take $/s/$ as a prefix are greater than $/s/$, so they belong to N and are the smallest in it. We use binary search in N again and divide N into two parts, O and P (shown in Fig. 3(c)). Indexes in O take $/s/$ as a prefix, and indexes in P do not. Note all indexes in O (exclude the last one) as *Middleindex*. So all records in the sub-trees that *Middleindex* point to take $/s/$ as a prefix. The process is called pre-scan because we distinguish *Middleindex* in a node without searching the sub-trees *Middleindex* point to. Note the last index of M and the last index of O as *Borderindex*. Recursively pre-scan the inner nodes that *Borderindex* point to with two-step binary search until leaves.

Complexity. If the number of records in the tree is N, each node has an average of m indexes, and there are k records that take $/s/$ as a prefix. The time complexity of the two-step binary is $O(\log_2 m)$, two-step binary search will be invoked at most $2 * \log_m N$ times in pre-scan. So the time complexity of pre-scan is $O(\log_2 N)$. The size of sub-tree to cut is $O(k)$. So the time complexity of *pre-scan prefix deletion* is $O(k + \log_2 N)$.

3.3   Key Replacement

In *pre-scan prefix deletion*, we cut out the sub-tree and release the memory of the indexes. So we get a series of leaves containing all target records, which are organized in a linked list. Let *first* be the head of the linked list, *last* be the tail, and note the linked list as *[first, last]*. We replace the prefix $/s$ to $/z$ of all records in *[first, last]* in this step.

3.4   Floating-Split Bulk Insertion

The striped linked list in Fig. 4(a) is *[first, last]*. In *floating-split bulk insertion*, we insert *[first, last]* into the tree and construct indexes that point to leaves in it with floating-split in the bottom-up direction. *Floating-split bulk insertion* consists of two steps.

In the first step, we find the position to insert *[first, last]* by searching $/z$, then split the leaf where $/z$ should locate and insert *[first, last]* to the split point (shown in Fig. 4(b)).

The second step is to construct and insert indexes that point to leaves in *[first, last]* (shown in Fig. 4(c) and (e)). In *floating-split bulk insertion* we do not search from the root to find the locations to insert indexes one by one. Instead, we search the leaf ahead of *first* and construct an array called *history* that records the internal nodes visited during searching. We keep a variable called *ordered* to record the split elements in *history*. Taking *ordered* as one for example (in Fig. 4(c)), it means that the last node in *history* has split, and the other nodes in *history* is *unordered*.

Inserting an index into an *unordered* node with binary search if it is not oversized after insertion (marked as N_3 in Fig. 4(c)). For the node that will be oversized after insertion (marked as N_1 in Fig. 4(c)), we take four steps: ① divide

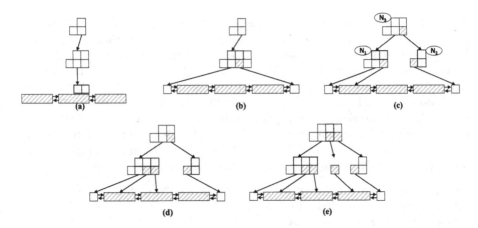

Fig. 4. *Floating-split bulk insertion* procedure. We insert the linked list into the tree in (a)–(b), and construct indexes that point to leaves in it in (c)–(e).

the indexes into two parts according to where the inserting index should locate, ② move the indexes in the right part to a new node (marked as N_2 in Fig. 4(c)), ③ append the inserting index to the end of N_1 and increase *ordered* by one and ④ insert an index that points to N_2 to the upper level (the previous node in *history*) by floating-split.

When inserting an index into an *ordered* node, we do not use binary search to find the position for insertion. Instead, we directly append it to the end of the *ordered* node (shown in Fig. 4(d)). If there is no sufficient space for appending (shown in Fig. 4(e)), three steps are taken: ① create a new node to replace the old in *history*, ② append the inserting index to the new node and ③ insert an index that points to the new node to the upper level (the previous node in *history*) by floating-split.

We judge whether a node is ordered by the variable *ordered*. Because *ordered* would not decrease, so we only split at most one time in each level. Compared with inserting an index into an *unordered* node, it is more efficient to append the index because it avoids the movement of elements. We call it floating-split because the nodes are split level by level with the variable *ordered*.

Modify Wrong Index. We modify a wrong index in an internal node without re-balancing overhead. Figure 5 depicts this procedure. *History* is marked by *line* in Fig. 5, in which are the positions that floating-split use to split internal nodes. The striped linked list is *[first, last]*, whose records noted as */keys*. */key1* is the previous record of *first*, and */key2* is the next of *last*. The node contains */keym* is the lowest common ancestor of */key1* and */key2* (*/key2* is in the sub-tree that */keym* points to). The lexicographical order of them is */key1* < */keym* ⩽ */key2* and */key1* < */keys* < */key2*. We insert the indexes that point to leaves in *[first, last]* before */keym* (*/keym* is on the right side of *line*), so there should be */keys*

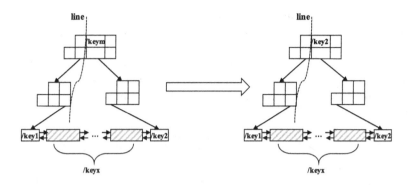

Fig. 5. Modify wrong index

$< /keym$. However, it is uncertain whether $/keys$ is less than $/keym$ or not. So we modify $/keym$ to $/key2$ before floating-split.

Complexity. Because the time cost of split and insertion is $O(\log_2 N)$, and $O(k)$ for appending. So the time complexity of *floating-split bulk insertion* is $O(k + \log_2 N)$.

3.5   Generalization

In Kyoto Cabinet, a node is legal as long as it contains an index, which simplifies *pre-scan prefix deletion* and *floating-split bulk insertion*. However, in classical B+-tree with an order of m, a node is illegal when the number of indexes in it is less than $m/2$. We explain how to expand *prefix replacement* to classical B+-tree in this section.

In *pre-scan prefix deletion*, the illegal nodes only occur on the left and the right border of the sub-tree to remove, which can be recorded in *pre-scan prefix deletion* and handled later, and the number of nodes on the border is $2 * \log_m N$. In *floating-split bulk insertion*, the illegal nodes only occur on the split nodes and *history*. There are $2 * \log_m N$ of these kinds of illegal nodes at most. These illegal nodes could be recorded and handled easily.

4   Evaluation

Experiment Environment. All results are collected on a machine with Xeon(R) E5-2680 (a 48-core 2.50 GHz Intel Core CPU) and 378 GB RAM. It runs CentOS 7.3.1611, 64-bit, with Linux kernel version 3.10.0.

Benchmarks and Configuration. We select two benchmarks, Mdtest [18] and Linux-4.20-rc5 [19]. We use Mdtest to generate a directory with about 100 million files/directories and select four directories to test, which contains 0.64,

3.84, 19.84 and 99.84 million files/directories respectively. We also use Linux-4.20-rc5, a version of Linux source code, to measure small workload which is more general in practice. There are 70492 files in it, and nine directories are selected for testing. The numbers of files/directories under them are 10, 107, 216, 418, 1127, 1951, 5182, 17030 and 26552. To calculate the execution time on Linux-4.20-rc5 more accurately, we run the tests 100 times.

Mechanism. The inefficiency of renaming directories exists in many full-path indexing file systems, including LocoFS, TokuFS, BetrFS and TABLEFS. These file systems use similar method, removing old records and set new records one by one, to implement renaming directories. So we extract the operations of LocoFS on database while recursively removing, recursively copying, renaming directories, and compare the performance with *pre-scan prefix deletion* and *floating-split bulk insertion* respectively.

We compare the execution time in each test, and calculate the breakdown to support that pre-scan and floating-split mechanisms eliminate most redundant search and compare cost.

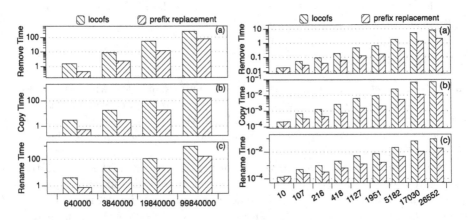

Fig. 6. Execution time in Mdtest   **Fig. 7.** Execution time in Linux-4.20-rc5

4.1   Remove

To evaluate *pre-scan prefix deletion*, we measure removing a directory recursively in this section. We cut out the sub-tree with pre-scan, then release the memory of records and leaves in it.

Execution Time. Figure 6(a) depicts that it is 3.32–4.42× faster than LocoFS to remove directories recursively in Mdtest benchmark. Figure 7(a) depicts that it is 0.98–4.09× faster than LocoFS to remove directories recursively in Linux-4.20-rc5.

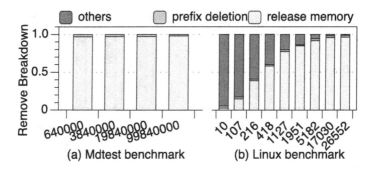

Fig. 8. Remove breakdown

Breakdown. Figure 8(a) depicts that it takes more than 96.9% of the time to release the memory of records and leaves, less than 3.0% for pre-scan in Mdtest benchmark. Figure 8(b) depicts that it takes 2.6% of the time to release the memory of records and leaves when the directory size is 10 in Linux-4.20-rc5. The percentage increases quickly and it reaches to 96.3% when the directory size is 26,552. It takes most of the time to release memory when removing a large directory recursively.

4.2 Copy

To test the performance of *floating-split bulk insertion*, we measure copying a directory */s* to */z* recursively in this section. Different with *prefix replacement*, we do not cut out the sub-tree with *pre-scan prefix deletion* to get target records. Instead, we ① use two-step binary search to find the leaf *first* and *last*, ② copy the target records in *[first, last]* to a new linked list, ③ replace the prefix of the records in the new linked list from */s* to */z* and ④ insert the new linked list into the tree and construct indexes that point to leaves in it by *floating-split bulk insertion*.

Execution Time. Figure 6(b) depicts that it is 4.51–5.64× faster than LocoFS to copy directories recursively in Mdtest benchmark. Figure 7(b) depicts that it is 0.95–6.27× faster than LocoFS to copy directories recursively in Linux-4.20-rc5.

Breakdown. Figure 9(a) depicts that it takes more than 90.1% of the time to construct records and little for floating-split in Mdtest benchmark. Figure 9(b) depicts that it takes 2.9% of the time to construct records when the directory size is 10 in Linux-4.20-rc5. The percentage increases quickly and it reaches to 97.4% when the directory size is 26,552. It takes most of the time to construct records when copying a large directory recursively.

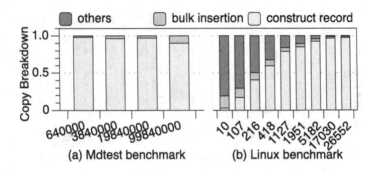

Fig. 9. Copy breakdown

4.3   Rename

To test the performance of *prefix replacement*, we measure renaming directories in this section.

Execution Time. Figure 6(c) shows that it is 5.01–5.52× faster than LocoFS to rename directories in Mdtest benchmark. Figure 7(c) depicts that it is 0.86–5.85× faster than LocoFS to rename directories in Linux-4.20-rc5.

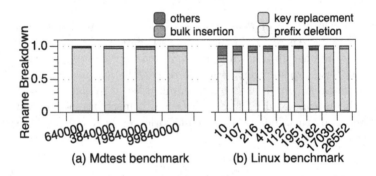

Fig. 10. Rename breakdown

Breakdown. Figure 10(a) shows that it takes 92.2% of the time for *key replacement* at least in Mdtest benchmark. Figure 10(b) depicts that it takes 4.8% of the time for *key replacement* when the directory size is 10 in Linux-4.20-rc5. The percentage increases quickly and it reaches to 93.8% when the directory size is 26,552. It takes most of the time for *key replacement* when renaming a large directory.

5   Conclusion

In this work, we present a *prefix replacement* interface in B+-tree to implement efficient renaming in full-path-indexed file systems, which eliminates most unnecessary search cost. The time complexity drops from $O(k * \log_2 N)$ to $O(k + \log_2 N)$.

The tests show that *pre-scan prefix deletion* and *floating-split bulk insertion* mechanisms beat LocoFS greatly when the directory size is greater than 100, and the performance is almost same when the directory size is about 10. Under the tests, we find that ① the cost of *pre-scan prefix deletion* mainly comes from release the memory of removed records and leaves, ② the cost of *floating-split bulk insertion* mainly comes from construction of new records and leaves and ③ the cost of *prefix replacement* mainly comes from *key replacement*, which proves that we reduce the search and compare cost successfully.

6   Future Work

Kyoto Cabinet stores keys and values continuously in records. So we cannot modify the key without changing the value, which makes *key replacement* inefficient. We will implement *prefix replacement* in the database that separately stores keys and values, so only keys should be modified while renaming a directory. We discuss how to generalize *prefix replacement* (in Sect. 3.5), and will implement it in the future.

References

1. McKusick, M.K., Joy, W.N., Leffler, S.J., Fabry, R.S.: A fast file system for UNIX. ACM Trans. Comput. Syst. **2**(3), 181–197 (1984)
2. Tao, X., Alei, L.: Small file access optimization based on GlusterFS. In: Proceedings of 2014 International Conference on Cloud Computing and Internet of Things, pp. 101–104 (2014)
3. Jannen, W., Yuan, J., Yang, Z., Esmet, J., Esmet, J., Jiao, Y.: BetrFS: a right-optimized write-optimized file system. In: 13th Conference on File and Storage Technologies, pp. 301–315 (2015)
4. Li, S., Lu, Y., Shu, J., Hu, Y., Li, T.: LocoFS: a loosely-coupled metadata service for distributed file systems. In: Proceedings of the International Conference for High Performance Computing, Networking, Storage and Analysis, pp. 4–15 (2017)
5. Esmet, J., Bender, M.A., Farach-Colton, M., Kuszmaul, B.C.: The TokuFS streaming file system. In: USENIX Conference on Hot Topics in Storage & File Systems (2012)
6. Jannen, W., Yuan, J., Zhan, Y., Akshintala, A., Esmet, J., Jiao, Y., et al.: BetrFS: write-optimization in a kernel file system. ACM Trans. Storage **11**(4), 1–29 (2015)
7. Ren, K., Gibson, G.A.: TABLEFS: enhancing metadata efficiency in the local file system. In: USENIX Annual Technical Conference, pp. 145–156 (2013)
8. Yuan, J., Zhan, Y., Jannen, W., Pandey, P., Akshintala, A., Chandnani, K., et al.: Optimizing every operation in a write-optimized file system. In: USENIX Conference on File & Storage Technologies (2016)

9. Zhan, Y., et al.: The full path to full-path indexing. In: Proceedings of the 16th USENIX Conference on File and Storage Technologies, pp. 123–138 (2018)
10. Ren, K., Zheng, Q., Patil, S., Gibson, G.: IndexFS: scaling file system metadata performance with stateless caching and bulk insertion. In: Proceedings of the International Conference for High Performance Computing, Networking, Storage and Analysis, pp. 237–248 (2014)
11. O'Neil, P., Cheng, E., Gawlick, D., O'Neil, E.: The log-structured merge-tree (LSM-tree). Acta Informatica **33**(4), 351–385 (1996)
12. Shetty, P.J., Spillane, R.P., Malpani, R.R., et al.: Building workload-independent storage with VT-trees. Presented as Part of the 11th USENIX Conference on File and Storage Technologies, pp. 17–30 (2013)
13. Sears, R., Ramakrishnan, R.: bLSM: a general purpose log structured merge tree. In: Proceedings of the 2012 ACM SIGMOD International Conference on Management of Data, pp. 217–228 (2012)
14. Brodal, G.S., Fagerberg, R.: Lower bounds for external memory dictionaries. In: Proceedings of the Fourteenth Annual ACM-SIAM Symposium on Discrete Algorithms, pp. 546–554 (2003)
15. Davies, A., Orsaria, A.: Scale out with GlusterFS. Linux J. **2013**(235), 1 (2013)
16. Patil, S., Gibson, G.A.: Scale and concurrency of giga+: file system directories with millions of files. In: USENIX Conference on File and Storage Technologies, vol. 11, p. 13 (2011)
17. Brandt, S.A., Miller, E.L., et al.: Efficient metadata management in large distributed storage systems. In: Mass Storage Systems and Technologies, pp. 290–298 (2003)
18. MDTEST Benchmark. https://github.com/MDTEST-LANL/mdtest. Accessed 16 Apr 2019
19. Linux release. https://git.kernel.org/pub/scm/linux/kernel/git/torvalds/linux.git/snapshot/linux-4.20-rc5.tar.gz. Accessed 16 Apr 2019
20. Lensing, P.H., Cortes, T., Hughes, J., Brinkmann, A.: File system scalability with highly decentralized metadata on independent storage devices. In: 2016 16th IEEE/ACM International Symposium on Cluster, Cloud and Grid Computing, pp. 366–375 (2016)
21. Shi, X., Lin, H., Jin, H., et al.: Giraffe: a scalable distributed coordination service for large-scale systems. In: 2014 IEEE International Conference on Cluster Computing, pp. 38–47 (2014)
22. Zheng, Q., Ren, K., Gibson, G., et al.: DeltaFS: exascale file systems scale better without dedicated servers. In: Proceedings of the 10th Parallel Data Storage Workshop, pp. 1–6 (2015)
23. Lensing, P.H., Cortes, T., Brinkmann, A.: Direct lookup and hash-based metadata placement for local file systems. In: Proceedings of the 6th International Systems and Storage Conference, p. 5 (2013)

Partition and Scheduling Algorithms for Neural Network Accelerators

Xiaobing Chen[1,2,3], Shaohui Peng[1,2,3], Luyang Jin[1,2,3], Yimin Zhuang[1,2,3], Jin Song[1,2,3], Weijian Du[1,2,3], Shaoli Liu[1], and Tian Zhi[1(✉)]

[1] SKL of Computer Architecture, Computing Technology, CAS, Beijing, China
{chenxiaobing,pengshaohui18z,zhuangyimin,songjin,duweijian,
liushaoli,zhitian}@ict.ac.cn
[2] University of Chinese Academy of Sciences, Beijing, China
[3] Cambricon Tech. Ltd., Shanghai, China
jinluyang@cambricon.com

Abstract. In recent years, Artificial Neural Networks have evolved rapidly and are applied to various fields. Meanwhile, to enhance computation efficiency of neural network applications, more and more neural network accelerators have been developed. Though traditional task scheduling algorithms on heterogeneous systems have been intensively researched, they can't be applied to neural network accelerators directly. Based on typical characteristics of neural network accelerators, we formalize the problem of tasks scheduling for neural networks, and transplant two listing heuristic scheduling algorithms, Heterogeneous-Earliest-Finish-Time (HEFT) and Critical-Path-on-a-Processor (CPOP). Inspired by the separable features of neural network operations, we propose two partition algorithms, the Iterative Partition Scheduling Algorithm (IPS) and the Partition Scheduling Combination Algorithm (PSC), which can be associated with scheduling algorithms. Further, we conduct experiments on some typical neural networks, and results show that compared to scheduling-only algorithms the partition associated algorithms achieve about 2x to 3x speedup.

Keywords: Neural network accelerators · Task partition · Scheduling algorithms

This work is partially supported by the National Key Research and Development Program of China (under Grant 2017YFB1003101), the NSF of China (under Grants 61432016, 61532016, 61672491, 61602441, 61602446, 61732002, 61702478, 61732007 and 61732020), Beijing Natural Science Foundation (JQ18013), the 973 Program of China (under Grant 2015CB358800), National Science and Technology Major Project (2018ZX01031102), the Transformation and Transfer of Scientific and Technological Achievements of Chinese Academy of Sciences (KFJ-HGZX-013), Key Research Projects in Frontier Science of Chinese Academy of Sciences (QYZDB-SSW-JSC001), Strategic Priority Research Program of Chinese Academy of Science (XDB32050200, XDC01020000) and Standardization Research Project of Chinese Academy of Sciences (BZ201800001).

© Springer Nature Switzerland AG 2019
P.-C. Yew et al. (Eds.): APPT 2019, LNCS 11719, pp. 55–67, 2019.
https://doi.org/10.1007/978-3-030-29611-7_5

1   Introduction

Artificial Neural Network is a very popular algorithm in machine learning fields. In recent years, along with the rapid development of deep learning technology, Artificial Neural-Network-based models and algorithms have made important breakthroughs in many fields. In the fields of speech [1], facial recognition [2], automatic driving [3] and machine translation [4], research works about algorithms based on deep neural networks are going deeper and deeper.

Unlike traditional algorithms, an important feature of deep neural networks is the coexistence of both high memory access and computational intensiveness. This is a huge challenge for general purpose processors. To face these challenges, mainstream neural network acceleration schemes can be roughly divided into three types. Graphics Processing Unit (GPU) [5], Field-Programmable Gate Array (FPGA) [6,7], and Application Specific Integrated Circuit (ASIC) [9]. GPUs feature their powerful parallel computing capability but face severe power efficiency problem, while FPGAs feature their flexibility but have poor peak performance. Unlike GPUs and FPGAs, ASICs are dedicated, customized hardware architectures. The multicore and in-memory computing [10,11] designs help them to outperform GPUs and FPGAs in terms of AI computing fields.

Task scheduling problem is a classical NP-hard problem [13], while it plays a key role in improving the overall system performance. Therefore, scheduling algorithms based on traditional applications and heterogeneous systems have been extensively studied [14]. Intrinsically, neural network accelerators can be regarded as a special class of heterogeneous systems, but the separability of neural network applications and customized function units for neural network accelerator make them quite different from the traditional applications and heterogeneous systems. As an emerging field, there are few researches on such task scheduling problems. In this paper, the corresponding task scheduling algorithms are studied for neural network applications and neural network accelerators.

The main contributions are summarized as followings.

1. **Modeling neural network accelerators and formalizing the task scheduling problem.** We summarize typical characteristics of existing neural network accelerators and abstract a general neural network accelerator model. Based on this model, we formalize the task scheduling problem combined with separability of neural networks.
2. **Transplanting scheduling algorithms and proposal of partition algorithms.** Since traditional scheduling algorithms can hardly be directly applied to neural network accelerators, we transplant two algorithms, HEFT and CPOP, into our accelerator model. To utilize the separability feature of neural networks, we propose two partition algorithms, IPS and PSC, adequately exploiting parallelism.
3. **Promising performance gain in typical neural network tasks.** In our self-built simulator, we conducted experiments on typical neural networks. Results show that compared to scheduling-only algorithms the partition associated algorithms achieve about 2x to 3x speedup.

The following sections are divided into 5 parts. Part I introduces related works on neural network accelerators and traditional task scheduling algorithms. Part II models the structure of the neural network accelerator and formalizes the scheduling problem about the neural network applications. Part III is the transplantation of traditional scheduling algorithms and we propose two improved scheduling algorithms based on partition strategy. Experiments and analysis are introduced in Part IV. Part V is a summary and a outlook for future work.

2   Related Work

2.1   Neural Network Accelerators

In order to meet the computation and memory intensive characteristics of neural network algorithms, and the demand for powerful computing resources, various solutions such as GPU, FPGA and ASIC have been extensively studied.

For GPUs, since neural network computing includes many stream computation and matrix operations, GPUs are frequently applied to neural network applications [5]. Meanwhile, GPUs have been added some neural network specific structures to improve the versatility, computation performance and power efficiency [15]. Compared to GPUs, FPGAs are much more efficient for everchanging neural network applications. Compared with ASICs, FPGAs overcome the shortcomings of long development cycle and poor scalability. Besides, FPGAs also provide acceptable computation performance. Therefore, there are many researches on FPGA-based neural network accelerators [8], like CNN dedicated accelerators [16]. Compared to GPUs and FPGAs, customized ASICs is a superior solution for the acceleration of neural network algorithms. Unlike traditional von Neumann architecture, ASICs typically use in-memory computational structures to improve memory usage efficiency [10,11].

To summarize the accelerators mentioned above, using multi-core, specialized neural network function units and enlarging on-chip communication bandwidth are common designs. For example, in order to accelerate the common neural network operations such as matrix multiplication, convolution, activation and pooling, the TPU proposed by Google is designed with various specialized modules such as matrix multiply unit, activation unit, and pool unit. Unified Buffer, and fast bandwidth between Host and Device are methods to optimize access efficiency [12]. Eyeriss [17] and Nullhop [18] are also neural network accelerators with similar architecture.

2.2   Task Scheduling Algorithms

Task scheduling algorithms based on heterogeneous systems have been extensively studied [14]. Since task scheduling is an NP-hard problem in most cases [13], various heuristic algorithms have been proposed.

List scheduling heuristic algorithms usually maintain a priority queue based on all tasks, and then cyclically performs task selection and processor selection until all tasks are scheduled. Mapping Heuristic (MH) [19], Earliest Time First (ETF) [20] are some examples of list scheduling heuristic algorithm. The two scheduling algorithms we transplanted in this paper, Heterogeneous-Earliest-Finish-Time (HEFT) and Critical-Path-on-a-Processor (CPOP) also belong to the list scheduling algorithm [14]. The Upward Rank and Downward Rank of each task are the most significant parts in these algorithms. Upward Rank refers to the shortest time required from the start of the mission to the current task. The Downward Rank is the shortest time from the current task to the end of the whole mission. The HEFT uses the upward rank as the priority to schedule tasks, while CPOP uses the sum of both to select and optimize the critical path.

But all traditional scheduling algorithms are based on the assumption that tasks cannot be separated into small parts and the processor is general to all tasks. Such a hypothesis is not consistent with the separability of neural network tasks and customized modules in neural network accelerators. Therefore, we first transplant traditional scheduling algorithms onto our abstracted neural network accelerator model, and further put forward split-based optimizations.

3   System Model and Problem Definition

In this section, we abstract a general configurable neural network accelerator model. Based on separability of neural networks and this model, we formalize the task scheduling problem.

3.1   The Configurable Neural Network Accelerators Model

According to computational characteristics, neural network operations can be divided into several types. For instance, Convolution and Full Connection Operations can be accomplished by matrix multiplication and reduce sum operation, Activation Operations can be accomplished by lookup tables. Neural network accelerators can obviously improve system performance by implementing operation specified function units exquisitely. Commonly heterogeneous systems communicate with assistance of main memory. Differently, function units in neural network accelerators often communicate with each other directly. With regard to neural network applications, dataflow transfer among function units directly, which don't need to be buffered. (see the neural network accelerator model as Fig. 1)

Demands for Neural Network Accelerators vary with different application scenarios. For edge computing fields, power efficiency and time delay are main focuses. While throughput and parallelism are the main ones for cloud servers. Basically, a Neural Network Accelerator model consists of series of function units and interconnected data transfer paths. Each function unit can accomplish several types of neural network operations. For example, both convolution and full connection operations could be accomplished by same kind of function units. The interconnected data transfer paths between each two function units could

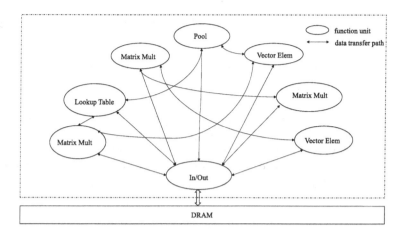

Fig. 1. A general model for neural network accelerators.

exist or not. In our model, the number, computational speed, connectivity and corresponding bandwidth of function units are all configurable parameters.

Assume neural network operations are divided into m sets, $op_1, op_2, \ldots, op_m$. Suppose a configured accelerator consists of n function units, $fu_1, fu_2, \ldots, fu_n$. For function unit fu_i, we use the function $g(fu_i)$ to represent the computation speed for function unit i, and function $h(fu_i, fu_j)$ to represent the bandwidth between fu_i and fu_j.

$$
h(fu_i, fu_j) = \begin{cases} b_{i,j} & the\ bandwidth\ equals\ to\ b_{i,j}, \\ \infty & i = j, \\ 0 & otherwise. \end{cases} \tag{1}
$$

3.2 Formulation of the Scheduling Problem

The neural network application can be represented by a directed acyclic graph (DAG), $G = (V, E)$. Each node $v_i \in V$ represents an operation and each edge $e_{i,j} \in E$ represents the data dependency between v_i and v_j. And node v_i can be executed on function unit fu_x if and only if $op(v_i) \in ops(fu_x)$, in which $op(v_i)$ means operation type of v_i, and $ops(fu_x)$ means the set of operation types supported on fu_x.

Assume the computation size is $cp(v_i)$, and the selected function unit $f(v_i)$. Then the computation time $cpt(v_i)$ can be reckoned out as $cp(v_i)/g(f(v_i))$. Assume the data transfer size from node v_i to node v_j is $io(v_i, v_j)$, and the corresponding transfer time $iot(v_i, v_j)$ is defined by $io(v_i, v_j)/h(f(v_i), f(v_j))$.

We introduce the conception of priority for nodes assigned to the same function unit. The priority of node v_i is $s(v_i)$. Nodes on the same function unit should be executed in priority order. We assume the start time of node v_i is $st(v_i)$, and the finish time is $ft(v_i)$. For nodes v_i and v_j on the same function unit, we have the following constraint.

$$st(v_i) >= ft(v_j) \quad if \ s(v_i) < s(v_j) \tag{2}$$

$$st(v_i) = \max\{ \max_{\substack{v_i \neq v_j \\ f(v_i)=f(v_j) \\ s(v_i)<s(v_j)}} ft(v_j), \ \max_{\substack{v_j \in pred(v_i) \\ f(v_i) \neq f(v_j)}} ft(v_j) + iot(v_j, v_i)\} \tag{3}$$

Specifically, for entry node v_i which has no predecessor, $st(v_i)$ equals to 0 or $ft(v_j)$ if v_j is also a entry node and $f(v_i)$ equals to $f(v_j)$. For other node, the start time is formulated as Eq. (3), and the finish time v_i is $ft(v_i) = st(v_i) + cpt(v_i)$.

Based on definitions above, the schedule problem is to find a function unit assignment function f and a priority setting function s to minimize the execution time.

$$\underset{s,f}{\operatorname{argmin}} \ \max_{v_i \in V} ft(v_i) \tag{4}$$

3.3 The Partition Associated Scheduling Problem

Most neural network operations can be accomplished by vectorized operations. Based on the weak data dependency, neural network operations can be partitioned to leverage task parallelism.

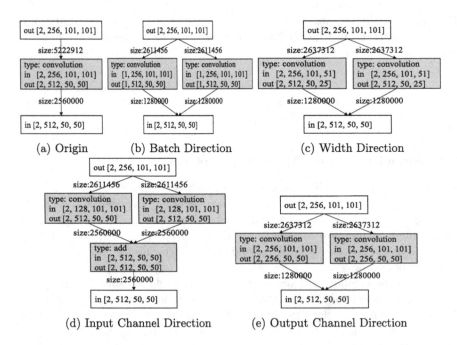

Fig. 2. Partition schemes for a convolution layer. In this case, the kernel is $512 \times 256 \times 3 \times 3$, the stride is 2×2. Compared with (a), (b) has the same computational size and data transfer size, (c) has an extra data transfer consumption (51712B), (d) has extra data transfer consumption (5120000B), and an extra add-supported function unit, while (e) has an extra data transfer consumption (5222912B).

Based on characteristics of different operations, we formulate partition strategies respectively. For example, based on the partition direction, a 2-D convolution operation can be partitioned by 5 ways. From the batch direction, no additional works involved, but if the batch number of application equals 1, this method can't work. From the input channel direction, an additional add operation is needed to add partial results from each partitioned child nodes. From the output channel direction, each child node needs to get full input, which will increase data transfer size. From the height or width direction, there could be additional data transfer consumption for overlapped inputs on each child nodes. (See Fig. 2) On the contrary, for a batch normalization operation, partition won't lead into additional workload. Similarly, we construct partition rules for each neural network operation.

For a partition procedure p_i, a node v would be replaced by new nodes and edges associated with v would be replaced by new edges. The data transfer size on new edges is tightly correlated with operation and parameters on it.

$$G'(V', E') = p_i(G(V, E)) \tag{5}$$

Assume we get a partition sequence $p = (p_1, p_2, \ldots, p_k)$, the partition associated schedule problem could be reformulated as follows:

$$\underset{p,s,f}{\operatorname{argmin}} \max_{v_i \in V} ft(v_i) \tag{6}$$

4   Partition and Scheduling Algorithms

In this section, we improve two algorithms, HEFT and CPOP, in terms of generality, so as to enable them to be used in our neural network accelerator model. To utilize the separability feature of neural networks, we propose two partition algorithms, IPS and PSC, adequately exploiting parallelism. Since the final result is measured by the cost model, these algorithms will always terminate with a practicable solution.

4.1   Transplanted Scheduling Algorithms

Because traditional scheduling algorithms can hardly apply to neural network accelerators, we improve HEFT and CPOP algorithms to adopt neural network applications. The improved HEFT algorithm firstly sets the priority of each node v_i with the Upward Rank value $rank_u(v_i)$ [14], which is calculated from mean computation time $\overline{cpt(v_i)}$ and mean communication time $\overline{iot(v_i, v_j)}$ in which v_j is a successor node of v_i. Different from original definition, $\overline{cpt(v_i)}$ and $\overline{iot(v_i, v_j)}$ in our algorithm is redefined as follows:

In Eqs. (7) and (8), n_i means the number of function units which support v_i.

In original CPOP algorithm, nodes in the critical path must use the same processor. But in the improved algorithm, we loose this constraint that nodes with the same type must be assigned to the same function unit.

$$\overline{cpt(v_i)} = cp(v_i) \cdot n_i / \sum_{op(v_i) \in ops(fu_j)} g(fu_j) \tag{7}$$

$$\overline{iot(v_i, v_j)} = io(v_i, v_j) \cdot n_i \cdot n_j / \sum_{\substack{op(v_i) \in ops(fu_x) \\ op(v_j) \in ops(fu_y)}} h(fu_x, fu_y) \tag{8}$$

4.2   The Iterative Partition Scheduling Algorithm (IPS)

Compared to traditional scheduling tasks, neural networks have less branches and more separability. To increase the opportunities of scheduling, we introduce the partition procedure to enhance the parallelism of neural network applications. We proposed a partition algorithm IPS that is applicable for most kinds of scheduling algorithms. In IPS, we firstly run the scheduling algorithm to get a critical path for the application. Then, we try to partition a node in the path to minimize scheduling time, which can get a local optimal partition strategy. By iteratively scheduling and partition, the neural network could be scheduled much more efficiently. Besides, we use a predefined minimal iteration number to prevent early stopping caused by local optimal solution.

4.3   The Partition Scheduling Combination Algorithm (PSC)

Compared to IPS, we propose a more aggressive partition algorithm PSC, which is a three-stage algorithm. Firstly, it partitions nodes in the original graph into child nodes evenly. Secondly, it schedules the partitioned graph by a specific scheduling algorithm. Finally, it tries to combine child nodes assigned to the same function units to decrease cost of partition.

To exploit the parallelism of neural network applications as much as possible, we use a partition stage to split each node into child nodes. Intuitively, these child

---

Algorithm 1. The Iterative Partition Scheduling Algorithm

---

1 set optimal makespan to $ms = \infty$ and iteration number $iter = 1$;
2 **do**
3   schedule $G(V, E)$ by a specific algorithm to get makespan mt;
4   find the critical path of $G(V, E)$;
5   initialize gain and target node, $gain = \infty$, $n_{opt} = n_1$;
6   **for** *node n_i in the critical path* **do**
7   try to split n_i and estimate gain gt;
8   update gain of split node $gain$ and critical node n_{opt};
9   **end**
10   update $G(V, E)$ to $G'(V', E')$ by splitting critical node n_{opt} evenly;
11   update $G(V, E)$ by $G'(V', E')$, $\nabla(m) = mt - ms$, $ms = max(ms, mt)$ and increase $iter$ by 1;
12 **while** $iter < iter_threshold$ *or* $\nabla(m) > makespan\_threshold$;
13 **return** $G'(V', E')$

Algorithm 2. The Partition Scheduling Combination Algorithm

---

1 **for** $v_i \in V$ **do**
2   get the number of function units n_i that support v_i;
3   split v_i into n_i child nodes evenly;
4 **end**
5 update $G(V, E)$ to $G'(V', E')$;
6 schedule $G'(V', E')$;
7 **for** *each function unit* fu_i **do**
8   try to combine nodes in fu_i;
9 **end**
10 **return** $G'(V', E')$

---

nodes could be scheduled into different function units and be executed parallelly. Since the partition procedure could introduce additional data transmission or computational costs, a node combination stage is applied to combine child nodes to eliminate unnecessary costs.

5 Experiments and Analysis

In this section, to verify the efficiency of our proposed algorithms, we conduct extensive simulated experiments with several classical neural networks. The algorithms includes the improved algorithms, HEFT and CPOP, and our proposed partition algorithms IPS and PSC. Then we show the result and analysis of these experiments.

5.1 Experimental Setup

We implement our experiment on a simulator, which consists of different types of function units. In addition to their types, the number of function units in different types, the computation speed, the topology relation and the bandwidth between these function units, are all configurable.

In the experiments, we use the following three metrics to show effect of our algorithms.

Makespan: Execution time of the scheduled neural network.

Speedup: The ratio of makespan to the minimum sequential execution time for a neural network. In our model, the sequential execution time is computed by assigning layers of the same operation to a function unit that minimizes the cumulative time of computation and data transmission costs.

Critical Hardware Occupy Rate (CHOR): We define critical function units as a class of function units which have the maximum occupy rate. This metric can be used to depict characters of different neural networks, such as distributions for different operations, and efficiency of a specific accelerator to an application.

5.2 Experimental Results

Scheduling-Only Algorithms. In our simulator, we set the number of function units for each operation type as 4. As shown in Fig. 3, for neural networks without branches, since no two layers could run in parallel, the speedup equals to 1. Neural networks with branches are also restrained by the limited parallelism of branches. So, scheduling the order of layers without leveraging intra-layer parallelism can't make full use of accelerators' parallelism.

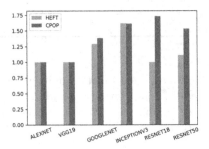

Fig. 3. Speedup for each neural network scheduled with HEFT and CPOP algorithms, on a simulator with 4 function units for each kind of operations.

Table 1. Results on typical neural networks for partition scheduling algorithms.

Neural network	Makespan	Speedup				CHOR			
		IPS		PSC		IPS		PSC	
		HEFT	CPOP	HEFT	CPOP	HEFT	CPOP	HEFT	CPOP
ALEXNET	58011.9	4.629	1.786	2.414	2.414	0.647	0.533	0.448	0.448
VGG16	71283.2	4.066	2.096	3.084	3.084	0.604	0.498	0.529	0.529
VGG19	81882.7	3.548	2.815	3.223	3.223	0.583	0.462	0.607	0.607
GOOGLENET	42122.2	3.668	3.351	3.245	2.973	0.857	0.417	0.981	0.899
INCEPTIONV3	100591	3.339	3.816	4.803	3.220	0.821	0.516	0.821	0.954
RESNET18	35416.2	3.231	2.188	2.721	2.626	0.769	0.521	0.769	0.521
RESNET50	38629.7	1.932	1.406	2.900	2.729	0.472	0.374	0.472	0.374

Iterative Partition Algorithms. We use the Iterative Scheduling Partition Algorithm associated with CPOP and HEFT respectively. As shown in Table 1, with 4 function units per kind, speedup for Alexnet with HEFT could reach 4.63. The main speedup interval is [3.2, 4.6] for HEFT, and [2.0, 3.8] for CPOP. The critical path estimated by CPOP is valid if and only if the accelerator has enough function units. Otherwise, it could shrink the search space and miss some potential optimization opportunities. While HEFT makes no such assumption, and search optimization greedily. And the experimental results also show that HEFT performs better than CPOP. The value of CHOR is mainly affected by the structure of neural networks, the organization of accelerator and scheduling algorithms. And as shown in the Table 1, CHOR value is positively correlated with Speedup value. GOOGLENET and INCEPTIONV3 show better performance than other networks with HEFT scheduling algorithm. With the Iterative Schedule Partition algorithm, the CHOR for most neural networks are greater than 45%, and the most efficient one could reach 85%.

The iteration number is of great significant. Also shown in Fig. 4, With the increase of iteration number, speedup has a increasing trend and converges to a value. The iteration number for typical neural networks is around 30.

Partition Scheduling Combination Algorithms. As shown in Table 1, the distribution of Speedup and CHOR value of PSC is similar to that of IPS. The Speedup value of HEFT approximately lies in [2.7, 3.3], while [2.6, 3.2] for CPOP. And In some cases, PSC shows better performance than IPS such as INCEPTIONV3 and RESNET50, which implies that IPS algorithm may get trapped in local optimum for some cases. Since PSC is a pretty aggressive algorithm which benefits from simple structures of neural networks, it is highly applicable to such scenarios.

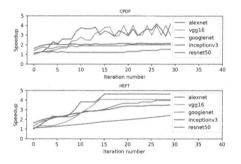

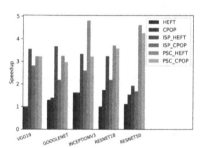

Fig. 4. A general model for neural network accelerators.

Fig. 5. Comparison of speedup of different kinds of algorithms.

Comparison. We compare Speedup values for various algorithms in most neural networks (see Fig. 5) in the simulator with 4 function units for each operation type, and find that partition associated scheduling algorithms promote performance apparently. In most cases, 2x–3x times performance improvement are gained by partition algorithms. IPS performs much more stably on most neural networks than PSC. But for very deep neural networks like RESNET50 and INCEPTIONV3, IPS is hard to converge to a global optimal point. Whereas aggressive algorithm like PSC may find a better solution directly.

6   Conclusions and Future Work

In this paper, we propose four scheduling algorithms which include improved HEFT, improved CPOP, IPS and PSC, to enhance system efficiency of neural network accelerators. In extensive comparison experiments with some popular and typical neural networks, we explicitly illustrate the superiority of our partition scheduling algorithms over scheduling-only algorithms and achieve about 2x to 3x speedup. We also perform a set of experiments to investigate the efficiency, robustness and stability of four scheduling algorithms.

In our future work, we will make efforts in the three aspects below: We will take hierarchical memory organizations into consideration, conduct experiments in more neural network applications and try to guide the design of neural network accelerators by scheduling results.

References

1. Amodei, D., et al.: Deep speech 2: end-to-end speech recognition in English and mandarin. In: International Conference on Machine Learning, pp. 173–182 (2016)
2. Taigman, Y., Yang, M., Ranzato, M., Wolf, L.: Deepface: closing the gap to human-level performance in face verification, pp. 1701–1708 (2014)
3. Bojarski, M., et al.: End to end learning for self-driving cars. arXiv: Computer Vision and Pattern Recognition (2016)
4. Bahdanau, D., Cho, K., Bengio, Y.: Neural machine translation by jointly learning to align and translate. In: International Conference on Learning Representations (2015)
5. Krizhevsky, A., Sutskever, I., Hinton, G.E.: Imagenet classification with deep convolutional neural networks. In: Neural Information Processing Systems, vol. 141, no. 5, pp. 1097–1105 (2012)
6. Gschwind, M.K., Salapura, V., Maischberger, O.: Space efficient neural net implementation (1994)
7. Ovtcharov, K., Ruwase, O., Kim, J.Y., Fowers, J., Strauss, K., Chung, E.S.: Accelerating deep convolutional neural networks using specialized hardware. Miscellaneous (2015)
8. Mittal, S.: A survey of FPGA-based accelerators for convolutional neural networks. Neural Comput. Appl. 1–31 (2018)
9. Rastegari, M., Ordonez, V., Redmon, J., Farhadi, A.: XNOR-Net: ImageNet classification using binary convolutional neural networks. In: Leibe, B., Matas, J., Sebe, N., Welling, M. (eds.) ECCV 2016. LNCS, vol. 9908, pp. 525–542. Springer, Cham (2016). https://doi.org/10.1007/978-3-319-46493-0_32
10. Sebastian, A., et al.: Temporal correlation detection using computational phase-change memory. Nat. Commun. 8(1), 1115 (2017)
11. Rios, C.E.C., et al.: In-memory computing on a photonic platform. Sci. Adv. 5(2), eaau5759 (2019)
12. Jouppi, N.P., Borchers, A., Boyle, R., Cantin, P.L., Nan, B.: In-datacenter performance analysis of a tensor processing unit (2017)
13. Ullman, J.D.: NP-complete scheduling problems. J. Comput. Syst. Sci. 10(3), 384–393 (1975)
14. Topcuoglu, H.R., Hariri, S., Wu, M.: Performance-effective and low-complexity task scheduling for heterogeneous computing. IEEE Trans. Parallel Distrib. Syst. 13(3), 260–274 (2002)
15. Mittal, S.: A survey on optimized implementation of deep learning models on the NVIDIA Jetson platform. J. Syst. Archit. 97, 428–442 (2019)

16. Zhang, C., Li, P., Sun, G., Guan, Y., Xiao, B., Cong, J.: Optimizing FPGA-based accelerator design for deep convolutional neural networks, pp. 161–170 (2015)
17. Chen, T., et al.: DianNao: a small-footprint high-throughput accelerator for ubiquitous machine-learning. ACM Sigplan Not. **49**(4), 269–284 (2014)
18. Aimar, A., et al.: NullHop: a flexible convolutional neural network accelerator based on sparse representations of feature maps. IEEE Trans. Neural Netw. **30**(3), 644–656 (2019)
19. Elrewini, H., Lewis, T.G.: Scheduling parallel program tasks onto arbitrary target machines. J. Parallel Distrib. Comput. **9**(2), 138–153 (1990)
20. Hwang, J., Chow, Y., Anger, F., Lee, C.: Scheduling precedence graphs in systems with interprocessor communication times. SIAM J. Comput. **18**(2), 244–257 (1989)

Optimization and Parallelization

SPART: Optimizing CNNs by Utilizing Both Sparsity of Weights and Feature Maps

Jiaming Xie[1,2(✉)] and Yun Liang[1,2]

[1] Peking University, Beijing, China
{jmxie,ericlyun}@pku.edu.cn
[2] Peng Cheng Laboratory, Shenzhen, China

Abstract. Intense convolution computation and great memory requirement in CNNs constraint their wider deployments and applications. Although both the weights and feature maps in CNNs can be sparse, directly mapping sparse convolution to spGEMM in HPC domain fails to improve the actual performance. Besides, existing sparse formats like CSR are not suitable for encoding the sparse feature maps because convolution operates across rows.

In this work, we propose a new format and a novel sparse convolution algorithm to optimize sparse CNNs on GPUs. First, we design the Compressed Feature Map (CFM) format to store the sparse feature maps. Second, we propose an efficient sparse convolution algorithm called SPART with sparse weights and sparse feature maps. Finally, we optimize this algorithm on GPUs. Our experiments show that our SPART algorithm has good performance. Compared with dense convolution, the speedup of SPART is up to **2.62×** (**1.77×** in average) on V100 and up to **1.84×** (**1.24×** in average) on Titan X.

Keywords: CNN · Sparse · Convolution · Format

1 Motivation

CNN (Convolution Neural Network) achieves great success in many domains, including computer vision [12], natural language processing [6], big data [4], etc. Compared with other deep neural networks, CNN introduces convolution layer to enhance the network's feature extraction ability, thus brings better performance. Meanwhile, convolution layers also brings much computation, making it the bottleneck of CNN computation performance.

Although CNNs have good performance in many applications, they are still not widely deployed. For example, because the storage, memory and computation requirement exceeds mobile devices' ability, it's hard to deploy CNNs to these devices [8]. There are many strategies to reduce the computation and storage

This work was supported by the National Natural Science Foundation China (No. 61672048).

© Springer Nature Switzerland AG 2019
P.-C. Yew et al. (Eds.): APPT 2019, LNCS 11719, pp. 71–85, 2019.
https://doi.org/10.1007/978-3-030-29611-7_6

requirement of CNNs, one of which is to prune the weights [8,16,28]. There are massive redundant weight parameters in CNNs, and pruning these weights out can safely reduce computation and storage requirements without reducing CNNs' accuracy. Meanwhile, input feature maps of convolution layers can be highly sparse as well owing to ReLU activation method [10], which turns non-positive values to zero.

Conventionally, the convolution operation is mapped to GEMM operation, because GEMM operation is highly optimized in HPC domain and can achieve good performance. Unfortunately, simply mapping sparse convolution to spGEMM hardly achieves speedup for several reasons. Firstly, the sparsity of weights and input feature maps fail to meet the requirement of spGEMM in HPC domain. In the University of Florida Sparse Matrix Collection [7] which is widely used as the benchmark of sparse matrix kernels in HPC domain, the typical matrices only have at most 1% or even less than 0.1% non-zero values, but the sparsity in convolution layers of CNNs, the weights and ifmaps have at least about 10% non-zero values. Secondly, mapping convolution to GEMM brings large memory overhead. The original input feature map will be unrolled into a larger matrix during the mapping, and in VGG [25] network whose convolution kernel size is 3 and stride is 1, the unrolled matrix is about 9× larger than the original feature map. In dense convolution, this overhead can be hided by computation-bound GEMM, but in sparse convolution, the unrolling overhead will badly worsen the performance of memory-bound spGEMM. In conclusion, owing to the insufficient sparsity and great memory overhead, simply mapping sparse convolution to spGEMM usually brings worse performance compared with the dense case.

As the most powerful acceleration device, GPU has been well studied and applied in many domains [14,15,29–32]. A few previous works try to utilize the sparsity in CNNs. [24] proposes direct sparse convolution method on CPUs to speedup sparse convolution between sparse weight kernels and dense input feature maps, and [3] implements this method on GPUs. However, to the best of our knowledge, no research has tried to utilize both the sparsity in weights and input feature maps.

In this work, we propose a novel sparse convolution algorithm for optimizing sparse CNNs on GPUs. To begin with, we try to utilize both the sparsity of weights and input feature maps. As the sparsity in convolution layers fails to meet the requirements of spGEMM in HPC domain and the existing sparse convolution methods don't support sparse feature maps, we design a novel sparse format to store the sparse input feature maps as well as new efficient sparse convolution algorithm. Furthermore, we implement the proposed algorithm on GPUs, and propose a finetuning model to guide the selection of the best SPART implementation across layers with different sparsity and parameters. The contributions of this work include:

1. We invent the Compressed Feature Map (CFM) format to store the sparse feature maps and provide assistance for spare convolution.
2. We design a new sparse convolution algorithm called SPART which operates on sparse weights and sparse feature maps.

3. We optimize the SPART algorithm on GPUs and finetune it to adapt to different layers. Compared with dense convolution, the speedup of SPART is up to 2.62× (1.77× in average) on V100 and up to 1.84× (1.24× in average) on Titan X.

2   Background

2.1   CNN and Convolution Operation

A typical CNN is a stack of different layers, such as convolution layers, fully connected layers, pooling layers, etc. The output of last layer becomes the input of next layer. Among all these layers, convolution layers are the computation bottleneck, because their convolution operations have intense computation [26].

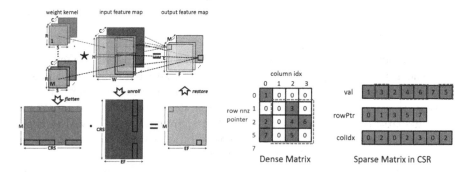

Fig. 1. Mapping high dimensional convolution to GEMM

Fig. 2. CSR format

Table 1. Shape parameters in convolution operation

Shape parameter	Description
N	batch size
M	# of output channels
C	# of input channels
R/S	weight kernel height/width
H/W	ifmap height/width
E/F	ofmap height/width

Each of the convolution layers in CNN is composed of high-dimensional convolutions as illustrated by Fig. 1. A group of *input feature maps* (ifmaps), each is called a *input channel*, conduct convolution with a group of *weight kernels* to get a single *output channel* of *output feature maps* (ofmaps). Different output channels of ofmaps are formed by different groups of weight kernels on the same group of ifmaps. A group of ifmaps is called a *batch*, different batches of ifmaps operate with same weight kernels to form different batches of ofmaps. In Fig. 1, there are C input channels, M output channels and 1 batch. Shape parameters in convolution operation are listed in Table 1.

The most common convolution implementation is to map convolution to GEMM. As illustrated by Fig. 1, all the weight kernels of the same output channel are flattened into a row, while the ifmap pixels in a same convolution operation are unrolled to a corresponding column. After the transformation, we multiply these two matrices to get the ofmap. As GEMM is highly optimized in HPC domain, mapping convolution to GEMM can achieve good performance, but it also requires much more memory than the size of original weights and ifmaps because unrolling the ifmap will greatly inflate its size. When it comes to sparse convolution, the memory overhead of GEMM method is severe enough to make sparse convolution less efficient than dense convolution.

2.2 Sparsity in CNN

In order to reduce the great number of weight parameters in CNN, many pruning methods have been proposed. As there are massive redundant parameters in CNN, [8] prune 90% weight values and greatly reduce the convolution computation. However, because the original regular structure of CNN is no longer kept and sparse convolution fails to meet the requirement of spGEMM in HPC domain (discussed in Sect. 1), the actual computation speed is not improved or even gets slower. Our work aims to solve this problem.

Besides weight sparsity, input feature maps are also sparse. ReLU, a popular activation method in CNN, turns non-positive feature map pixels to zeroes, which brings great sparsity to feature maps. What's more, the padding operation before convolution also brings zeroes. However, few researches try to utilize the sparsity in feature maps, and to our best knowledge, our work is the first to utilize both the sparsity in weights and feature maps in sparse convolution.

In HPC domain, there are many sparse matrix formats [2], such as CSR, COO, DIA, etc. Owing to limited space, we only introduce CSR format here. As shown in Fig. 2, there are three arrays in CSR format. Array *val* has nnz elements, which stores all the non-zero values in the original matrix. Array *rowPtr* has $row + 1$ elements, and its ith element points to the position of the first element in original matrix's i^{th} row. Array *colIdx* has nnz elements, which are the column indexes of corresponding non-zero value.

Sparse weights are suitable to be stored in CSR because values in the same kernel can be stored in the same row and can be accessed continuously. However, sparse feature maps don't have the same property. For example, as shown in Fig. 2, for a convolution area outlined in red dashed box, its non-zero values are not continuous as outlined in red boxes of the *val* array. This incontinuity makes CSR not suitable for sparse ifmaps, because we will have to search the entire row to locate the elements of the convolution area each time we switch between rows, which will bring much overhead. Therefore, we are supposed to design a new format to store sparse feature maps and design corresponding sparse convolution algorithm.

3   Format Design

3.1   Weight Compression

As shown in Fig. 3, we compress weight kernels with CSR format. First, we flatten the elements from the same output channel into a row, and rows from different output channels form a matrix. Then, we compress the flattened matrix in CSR format. For a weight pixel in $[m, c, r, s]$, its valPtr value is m, and its colIdx value is calculated as

$$colIdx_{m,c,r,s} = s + S(r + Rc) \tag{1}$$

In this way, for a pixel in m^{th} row with colIdx value $colIdx_{m,c,r,s}$, we are able to restore its location $[m, c, r, s]$ according to

$$
\begin{aligned}
s &= colIdx_{m,c,r,s} \bmod S \\
r &= \lfloor \frac{colIdx_{m,c,r,s}}{S} \rfloor \bmod R \\
c &= \lfloor \frac{colIdx_{m,c,r,s}}{SR} \rfloor
\end{aligned}
\tag{2}
$$

Because existing formats are not suitable for sparse ifmap, we design a new **Compressed Feature Map (CFM)** format for it.

3.2   CFM Overview

Our proposed sparse format CFM is illustrated by Fig. 3. As described in Table 1, we assume that the weight shape is $MCRS$, and the ifmap shape is $NCHW$. There are four arrays in the proposed format:

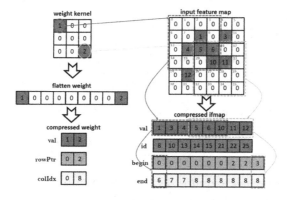

Fig. 3. Compression of weights and ifmaps

Array val stores all the non-zero values of the ifmap. This array has if_nnz elements.

Array id stores the ids of the corresponding values in array val. This array has if_nnz elements. In order to store the location information, all the pixels in the original ifmap are assigned with an id. In Fig. 3, ids are located in the top left corner of each pixel. The id of pixel [n, c, h, w] is defined as

$$id_{n,c,h,w} = w + W[h + H(c + Cn)] \tag{3}$$

In this definition, we are able to calculate any pixel's location $[n, c, h, w]$ from its id and pre-known ifmap size $NCHW$ as follows:

$$
\begin{aligned}
w &= id_{n,c,h,w} \bmod W \\
h &= \lfloor \frac{id_{n,c,h,w}}{W} \rfloor \bmod H \\
c &= \lfloor \frac{id_{n,c,h,w}}{WH} \rfloor \bmod C \\
n &= \lfloor \frac{id_{n,c,h,w}}{WHC} \rfloor
\end{aligned}
\tag{4}
$$

Array begin and array end store the range pointers of each weight pixel's computation area. Each of these two arrays has $NCRS$ elements. As shown in Fig. 3, each weight pixel has its own convolution computation area outlined by dashed rectangular. If we search the id array each time we start convolution computation for a weight pixel, we will suffer from great locating overhead. Therefore, we choose to record the computation area's range for each weight pixel. As one ifmap will be used by different weight kernels from different output channels, and non-zero values might appear in any position within the kernels, we are supposed to store the ranges for all the weight pixels. The computation range of the ith pixel in a weight kernel is recorded as $[begin[i],\ end[i])$. For example, in Fig. 3, the first weight pixel's computation range is $[0, 6)$. Detailed computation procedure will be introduced in Sect. 4.

3.3   CFM Analysis

CFM is Efficient in Compression. Our proposed format has a size of

$$S_{if} = 2if\_nnz + 2NCRS \tag{5}$$

and the compression rate is

$$comp\_rate = \frac{2if\_nnz + 2NCRS}{NCHW} = \frac{2if\_nnz}{NCHW} + \frac{2RS}{HW} \tag{6}$$

The storage for array val and id is necessary as they store vital information. It seems that the array $begin$ and end bring great memory overhead, but in convolution layers of real-world CNNs, the size of an single ifmap is much larger than the size of a weight kernel, which means $\frac{2RS}{HW}$ will be a small value. Therefore, the compression format is relatively efficient in size.

CFM is able to Provide Assistance for Continuous Computation and Workload Partition. The pointers stored in array *begin* and *end* points to continuous area in *val* and *id* which indicate the workload of a weight pixel, so the computation can be readily divided at the granularity of weight pixels. Section 5 provides more details on how CFM assists continuous computation and workload partition.

4   SPART Algorithm

Algorithm 1 presents the proposed sparse convolution algorithm (SPART) which takes sparse weights and sparse ifmaps as inputs, and output the dense ofmap. From line 1 to line 6, we get a non-zero value and its location from the compressed weight. In line 7, we compute the offset of this weight pixel's *begin* and *end* pointers, and access them in line 8. In line 9 and 10, the ids and values in the computation range are accessed for computation. In line 11, we compute the location of the computation result from the locations of weight pixel and ifmap pixel which are calculated according to the equations shown in Sect. 3. In line 12, the partial result is calculated and added to corresponding position of the ofmap.

Algorithm 1. SPART Algorithm

 1: **procedure** SPSPCONV(W, IF, OF)
 2:     **for** n in $[0, \text{N})$ **do**
 3:         **for** m in $[0, \text{M})$ **do**
 4:             **for** i in $[\text{W}.rowPtr[m], \text{W}.rowPtr[m+1])$ **do**
 5:                 $col = \text{W}.colIdx[i]$
 6:                 $w\_val = \text{W}.val[i]$
 7:                 $if\_off = col + n*\text{C}*\text{R}*\text{S}$
 8:                 **for** j in $[\text{IF}.begin[if\_off], \text{IF}.end[if\_off])$ **do**
 9:                     $if\_id = \text{IF}.id[j]$
10:                     $if\_val = \text{IF}.val[j]$
11:                     $of\_off = \text{ComputeOff}(col, id)$
12:                     $OF[of\_off] += if\_val * w\_val$
13:                 **end for**
14:             **end for**
15:         **end for**
16:     **end for**
17: **end procedure**

---

5 Implementation on GPUs

5.1 Parallelism

The parallelism strategy aims to increase concurrency, to reduce warp divergence and conflicts among thread blocks. With the assistance of the *begin* and *end* array in CFM format, we are able to directly divide the tasks between different weight pixels. As tasks in different batches are independent, they are simply assigned to different thread blocks. However, to get an output feature map, all the temporal results from different input channels have to be summed up, which requires atomic operations because all the input channels are computed concurrently. For example, in step 3 of Fig. 4, both task 1 and 2 write their temporal results to the ofmap concurrently. To reduce the overhead of atomic operations, we assign the tasks of the same output channel to a single thread block so that all the atomic operations are within the thread block and avoid synchronization across thread blocks. As for the memory and computation for redundant area, if we identify the redundant pixels and eliminate their computation, we will suffer from great warp divergence and memory alignment issues because the redundant pixels are scattered in the computation array. Therefore, we choose to calculate the redundant pixels as well and discard the redundant results after computation.

To put it together, as illustrated in Fig. 4, we assign the computations in different output channels and batches to different thread blocks. Within each thread block, the task is divided at the granularity of weight pixels, and within each task, the first step is to find the corresponding computation range pointers from *begin* and *end* arrays in the compressed ifmap. Then each task locates their own computation range, calculate the partial result and atomically add to the corresponding position of the result. As there are redundant pixels in the final result, after all the computations in the same thread block is completed, we finally write the required pixels back to the ofmap and discard the redundant pixels.

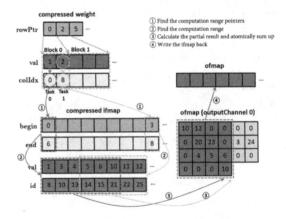

Fig. 4. Implementation on GPUs

5.2   Memory Optimization

As shown in Fig. 4, there are 7 input arrays and 1 output array in SPART, and their memory traces are different. For arrays in the compressed weight, their elements will only be accessed once and can be stored in the register file. As for the compressed ifmap, the accessed pixels' positions depend on weight information, which makes their visiting pattern irregular. Elements in array *begin* and *end* are only accessed once, and visited pixels are usually not continuous, so we simply load the visited pixels into the register files.

On the contrast, elements of *val* and *id* might be accessed more than once, and the visited pixels in a same task are continuous. Because the accesses to *val* and *id* are irregular and their elements might be reused, we cache these two arrays in L1 cache. Given the fact that the accessed pixels of ifmap's *val* and *id* in a same task are continuous and might be coalesced together when issued by memory, we assign a group of threads, say G threads, to compute a single task. The optimal number of G varies in different sparsity and convolution parameters, and we further discuss how to finetune it in Sect. 5.3.

For the output array, as the result pixels will be accessed for multiple times, and the size of result array in a block is small, they are placed in shared memory. After the computation is finished, threads in a block will write the required result pixels back to the ofmap array in global memory.

5.3   Finetuning Model

During computation, the G threads of the same task will load a continuous range of ifmap pixels at the same time to make use of coalescing. However, the threads who have no assigned pixel have to wait for other threads, which will bring divergence. More threads we assign to a single task, more memory access might be coalesced, but more greater the divergence problem will be. As the computation in a task might be influenced by the ifmap's sparsity and other convolution parameters such as weight's kernel size, ifmap's size, etc, the optimal thread number G varies across layers.

To finetune the number of G, we propose a model which takes both memory coalescing and thread divergence into consideration. The workload of a task is estimated as

$$W = EF(1 - s) \tag{7}$$

where EF is the size of an ofmap, s denotes the sparsity of the ifmap, and W denotes the workload of a single task. Considering memory coalescing, a task's memory accessing time is directly proportional to the workload of a task and reversely proportional to the concurrent thread number G as shown below:

$$T_{mem} = \frac{W P_{mem}}{G} \tag{8}$$

In Eq. 8, P_{mem} denotes the penalty of a single memory access, and T_{mem} denotes the task's memory accessing time.

As for divergence problem, the additional time brought by divergence is directly proportional to G which is described as:

$$T_{div} = GP_{div} \tag{9}$$

In Eq. 9, $P_{divergence}$ denotes the penalty of divergence. To put it together, the time brought by memory and divergence of a task T_{task} is

$$T_{task} = T_{mem} + T_{div} = \frac{EF(1-s)P_{mem}}{G} + GP_{div} \tag{10}$$

We can pre-run some batches (10 batches for example) to finetune the values of P_{mem} and P_{div}. After that, the parameters are fixed and we run the actual batches as demand.

6   Experiment

We evaluate the performance of SPART on two platforms: NVIDIA Tesla V100 [22] represents data-center platform, while NVIDIA GTX Titan X [21] represents desktop platform. We use three classic CNNs: AlexNet [12], VGG16 [25] and googLeNet [27] as our benchmarks. We only test the convolution layers of these CNNs and ignore other kinds of layers. To avoid overhead of DNN frameworks, we extract the weights and ifmaps from Caffe [11] with the trained models from Caffe Model Zoo[1] and inputs from ImageNet [12] Dataset, and do the convolutions in independent codes. We use gcc 5.0 and NVCC 9.0 for compilation. In the experiments, we adjust the sparsity of weights to 90% and ifmaps from 75% to 90%, then evaluate the performance in different sparsity levels. The used data type is 32-bit floating point, and the batch size is 128.

When mapping dense convolution to GEMM, we use the CUBLAS [18] library, and we use the CUSPARSE [20] library when mapping sparse convolution to spGEMM.

6.1   Finetuning Performance

To evaluate the performance of our finetuning model, we take several convolution layers from VGG16 as our benchmark, and their convolution parameters are listed at Table 2. Because these layers have different convolution parameters, they have different optimal G and are suitable to test the finetuning model. We adjust the weight at sparsity 90% while ifmap's sparsity is 75% and 90%. We implement SPART on Titan X with different G, and record their speed compared with dense GEMM method.

Experimental results are shown in Fig. 5. In Fig. 5, cublas denotes the dense GEMM method, and SPART_4 to SPART_32 denote SPART method with G equals 4 to 32. Red dots represent the selected SPART method by our finetuning model. We may have several observations from the result:

---

[1] https://github.com/BVLC/caffe/wiki/Model-Zoo.

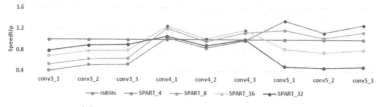

(a) weight sparsity 90%, ifmap sparsity 75%

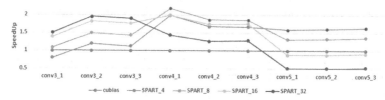

(b) weight sparsity 90%, ifmap sparsity 90%

Fig. 5. Finetuning on VGG layers

Table 2. VGG16 layer parameters

VGG16 layer	weight shape (MCRS)	ifmap shape (NCHW)	ofmap shape (NMEF)
conv3_1	(256, 128, 3, 3)	(128, 128, 56, 56)	(128, 256, 56, 56)
conv3_2	(256, 256, 3, 3)	(128, 256, 56, 56)	(128, 256, 56, 56)
conv3_3	(256, 256, 3, 3)	(128, 256, 56, 56)	(128, 256, 56, 56)
conv4_1	(512, 256, 3, 3)	(128, 256, 28, 28)	(128, 512, 28, 28)
conv4_2	(512, 512, 3, 3)	(128, 512, 28, 28)	(128, 512, 28, 28)
conv4_3	(512, 512, 3, 3)	(128, 512, 28, 28)	(128, 512, 28, 28)
conv5_1	(512, 512, 3, 3)	(128, 512, 14, 14)	(128, 512, 14, 14)
conv5_2	(512, 512, 3, 3)	(128, 512, 14, 14)	(128, 512, 14, 14)
conv5_3	(512, 512, 3, 3)	(128, 512, 14, 14)	(128, 512, 14, 14)

1. The optimal G for layers conv3_1 to conv3_3 is 32, while in layer conv5_1 to conv5_3 the optimal G is 8. The former layers are large enough to benefit from the memory coalescing, while the latter layers are so small that the divergence problem plays a more important role than benefit of memory coalescing. Our model successfully identifies the optimal G in these layers.
2. For layer conv4_1 to conv4_3, the optimal G is 16 when ifmap's sparsity is 75% while when ifmap's sparsity is 90%, the optimal G is 8. The difference comes from the workload change brought by sparsity variety, just as the case brought by layer size difference. Our model also successfully identifies the optimal G in these situations.
3. The speedup in Fig. 5b is much greater than ones in 5a. The sparser the ifmaps are, the less computation and memory SPART has, which brings better performance.

In conclusion, our finetuning model can identify the optimal G in different layers and different sparsity.

6.2   Overall Convolution Performance

The overall convolution performance of the three CNNs is shown in Fig. 6. We adjust the weight sparsity to 90%, and change the ifmap sparsity from 75% to 90%. In Fig. 6, cublas denotes the dense GEMM method, and cusparse denotes the spGEMM method. The direct sparse convolution method [24] with sparse weight and dense ifmap is denoted by spconv. SPART_8 and SPART_16 denote SPART implementations with G equals to 8 and 16 respectively, and SPART_tuned denotes SPART implementation with finetuned G in different layers. We may have several observations from Fig. 6 as below:

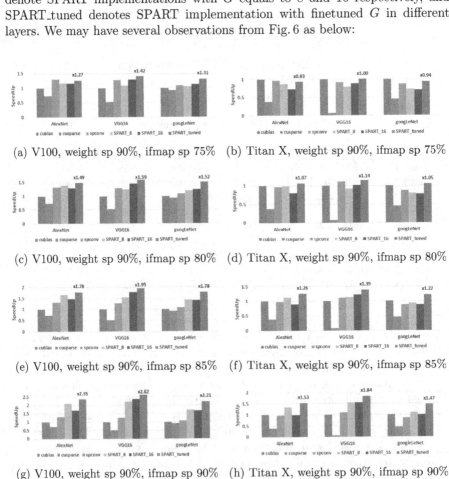

(a) V100, weight sp 90%, ifmap sp 75%   (b) Titan X, weight sp 90%, ifmap sp 75%

(c) V100, weight sp 90%, ifmap sp 80%   (d) Titan X, weight sp 90%, ifmap sp 80%

(e) V100, weight sp 90%, ifmap sp 85%   (f) Titan X, weight sp 90%, ifmap sp 85%

(g) V100, weight sp 90%, ifmap sp 90%   (h) Titan X, weight sp 90%, ifmap sp 90%

Fig. 6. Convolution speedup

1. Directly mapping sparse convolution to spGEMM, denoted by cusparse, is much slower than the original dense GEMM method in all conditions, which means it is extremely inefficient. The inefficiency comes from the inflated size of unrolled ifmap and the insufficient sparsity as discussed in Sect. 2.

2. The spconv only achieves slight speedup on V100 and almost no speedup on Titan X, because it only utilizes the sparsity in weights but ignores the ifmap sparsity.
   The SPART_8 and SPART_16 have moderate speedup in most cases, and their performances differ with each other in different sparsity and CNNs. In higher ifmap sparsity and smaller CNN such as AlexNet, the SPART_8 will have better performance because of the smaller workload, while in other cases SPART_16 is better. This is the reason why we must propose a finetuning model.

3. The SPART_tuned achieves high speedup in most cases. On V100, the speedup of SPART_tuned is up to **2.62×** and in average **1.77×**. On Titan X, the speedup of SPART_tuned is up to **1.84×** and in average **1.24×**.

In conclusion, our proposed SPART algorithm can achieve good performance in sparse CNNs.

7 Related Work

Convolution Algorithms. Besides GEMM, there are also other convolution methods. [17] maps convolution to Fast Fourier Transform (FFT) computation and reduces the computation's complexity, but this method can only applies to convolution layers with weight kernel 3×3. [13] transforms convolution to Winograd algorithm, but it also has some constraints for weight kernel size. CUDNN [19] library provides support to map dense convolution to these algorithms, and sparse convolution is not supported.

Sparse CNN Accelerators. Many recent works aim at accelerating sparse CNNs on hardware like FPGA and ASIC. EIE [9] compresses the parameters of fully connected layers in CNN to reduce storage and memory requirement as well as speedup inference. SCNN [23] conducts Cartesian product when mapping sparse convolution to spGEMM to help partition the workloads. Cambricon-X [33] applies step indexing technique to divide the non-zeroes in sparse convolution and achieve relatively balanced workload, while Eyeriss [5] gates the computation cycles for zero values in ifmap. Cnvlutin [1] proposes Zero-Free Neuron Array format to skip the multiplications of zero values in the ifmap.

8 Conclusion

CNN achieves great success in many domains, but its great computation requirement constraints its application. In this work, we propose SPART to accelerate sparse CNNs by utilizing both sparsity in weights and feature maps. First, we design a novel Compressed Feature Map (CFM) format to store the compressed feature maps and provide assistance for sparse convolution. Second, we propose the SPART algorithm which conducts sparse convolution on sparse weights and sparse feature maps. Finally, we implement SPART on GPUs and propose a finetuning model to optimize its performance. Compared with original dense convolution, the speedup of SPART is up to $2.62\times$ and in average $1.77\times$ On V100. On Titan X, the speedup of SPART is up to $1.84\times$ and in average $1.24\times$. In future, we plan to map sparse convolution to sparse FFT or Winograd to reduce computation complexity and achieve greater speedup.

Acknowledgement. This work was supported by the National Natural Science Foundation China (No. 61672048).

References

1. Albericio, J., Judd, P., Hetherington, T., Aamodt, T., Jerger, N.E., Moshovos, A.: Cnvlutin: ineffectual-neuron-free deep neural network computing. SIGARCH Comput. Archit. News **44**(3), 1–13 (2016). https://doi.org/10.1145/3007787.3001138
2. Bell, N., Garland, M.: Implementing sparse matrix-vector multiplication on throughput-oriented processors. In: SC 2009, p. 11. ACM, New York (2009). https://doi.org/10.1145/1654059.1654078. Article 18
3. Chen, X.: Escort: efficient sparse convolutional neural networks on GPUs. CoRR abs/1802.10280 (2018). arXiv:1802.10280
4. Chen, X.W., Lin, X.: Big data deep learning: challenges and perspectives. IEEE Access **2**, 514–525 (2014). https://doi.org/10.1109/ACCESS.2014.2325029
5. Chen, Y., Emer, J., Sze, V.: Eyeriss: a spatial architecture for energy-efficient dataflow for convolutional neural networks. In: ISCA 2016, pp. 367–379 (2016). https://doi.org/10.1109/ISCA.2016.40
6. Collobert, R., Weston, J., Bottou, L., Karlen, M., Kavukcuoglu, K., Kuksa, P.: Natural language processing (almost) from scratch. J. Mach. Learn. Res. **12**, 2493–2537 (2011). http://dl.acm.org/citation.cfm?id=1953048.2078186
7. Davis, T.A., Hu, Y.: The University of Florida sparse matrix collection. ACM Trans. Math. Softw. **38**(1), 25 (2011). https://doi.org/10.1145/2049662.2049663. Article 1
8. Han, S., et al.: Deep compression: compressing deep neural networks with pruning, trained quantization and Huffman coding. In: ICLR (2015)
9. Han, S., et al.: EIE: efficient inference engine on compressed deep neural network. CoRR abs/1602.01528 (2016). arXiv:1602.01528
10. He, K., Zhang, X., Ren, S., Sun, J.: Delving deep into rectifiers: surpassing human-level performance on ImageNet classification. CoRR abs/1502.01852 (2015). arXiv:1502.01852
11. Jia, Y., et al.: Caffe: convolutional architecture for fast feature embedding. In: MM (2014)
12. Krizhevsky, A., Sutskever, I., Hinton, G.E.: ImageNet classification with deep convolutional neural networks. In: NIPS (2012)
13. Lavin, A.: Fast algorithms for convolutional neural networks. CoRR abs/1509.09308 (2015). arXiv:1509.09308
14. Li, X., Liang, Y., Yan, S., Jia, L., Li, Y.: A coordinated tiling and batching framework for efficient GEMM on GPUs. In: PPoPP 2019, pp. 229–241. ACM, New York (2019). https://doi.org/10.1145/3293883.3295734

15. Li, X., et al.: cuMBIR: an efficient framework for low-dose X-ray CT image reconstruction on GPUs. In: ICS 2018, pp. 184–194. ACM, New York (2018). https://doi.org/10.1145/3205289.3205309
16. Luo, J.H., Wu, J., Lin, W.: ThiNet: a filter level pruning method for deep neural network compression. CoRR abs/1707.06342 (2017). arXiv:1707.06342
17. Mathieu, M., Henaff, M., LeCun, Y.: Fast training of convolutional networks through FFTs. CoRR abs/1312.5851 (2013). arXiv:1312.5851
18. NVIDIA: cuBLAS Library (2018a). https://docs.nvidia.com/cublas
19. NVIDIA: cuDNN Library (2018b). https://developer.nvidia.com/cudnn
20. NVIDIA: cuSPARSE Library (2018c). https://docs.nvidia.com/cusparse
21. NVIDIA: GTX Titan X: a desktop GPU (2018d). https://www.geforce.com/hardware/desktop-gpus/geforce-gtx-titan-x
22. NVIDIA: v100: a data-center GPU for AI (2018e). https://www.nvidia.com/en-us/data-center/tesla-v100/
23. Parashar, A., et al.: SCNN: an accelerator for compressed-sparse convolutional neural networks. CoRR abs/1708.04485 (2017). arXiv:1708.04485
24. Park, J., Li, S.R., Wen, W., Li, H., Chen, Y., Dubey, P.: Holistic SparseCNN: forging the trident of accuracy, speed, and size. CoRR abs/1608.01409 (2016). arXiv:1608.01409
25. Simonyan, K., Zisserman, A.: Very deep convolutional networks for large-scale image recognition. CoRR abs/1409.1556 (2014). arXiv:1409.1556
26. Sze, V., Chen, Y.-H., Yang, T.-J., Emer, J.S.: Efficient processing of deep neural networks: a tutorial and survey. CoRR abs/1703.09039 (2017). arXiv:1703.09039
27. Szegedy, C., et al.: Going deeper with convolutions. In: CVPR (2015)
28. Wen, W., Wu, C., Wang, Y., Chen, Y., Li, H.: Learning structured sparsity in deep neural networks. CoRR abs/1608.03665 (2016). arXiv:1608.03665
29. Xie, X., Liang, Y., Li, X., Tan, W.: CuLDA: solving large-scale LDA Problems on GPUs. In: HPDC 2019, pp. 195–205. ACM, New York (2019). https://doi.org/10.1145/3307681.3325407
30. Xie, X., et al.: Enabling coordinated register allocation and thread-level parallelism optimization for GPUs. In: MICRO 2015, pp. 395–406 (2015a). https://doi.org/10.1145/2830772.2830813
31. Xie, X., Liang, Y., Wang, Y., Sun, G., Wang, T.: Coordinated static and dynamic cache bypassing for GPUs. In: HPCA 2015, pp. 76–88 (2015b). https://doi.org/10.1109/HPCA.2015.7056023
32. Xie, X., Tan, W., Fong, L.L., Liang, Y.: CuMF_SGD: parallelized stochastic gradient descent for matrix factorization on GPUs. In: HPDC 2017, pp. 79–92. ACM, New York (2017). https://doi.org/10.1145/3078597.3078602
33. Zhang, S., et al.: Cambricon-X: an accelerator for sparse neural networks. In: MICRO 2016, pp. 1–12 (2016). https://doi.org/10.1109/MICRO.2016.7783723

DA-BERT: Enhancing Part-of-Speech Tagging of Aspect Sentiment Analysis Using BERT

Songwen Pei[1,2,3(✉)], Lulu Wang[1], Tianma Shen[1], and Zhong Ning[2]

[1] School of Optical-Electrical and Computer Engineering,
University of Shanghai for Science and Technology, Shanghai 200093, China
swpei@usst.edu.cn
[2] School of Management, Fudan University, Shanghai 200433, China
[3] State Key Laboratory of Computer Architecture, Institute of Computing
Technology, Chinese Academy of Sciences, Beijing 100190, China

Abstract. With the development of Internet, text-based data from web have grown exponentially where the data carry large amount of valuable information. As a vital branch of sentiment analysis, the aspect sentiment analysis of short text on social media has attracted interests of researchers. Aspect sentiment classification is a kind of fine-grained textual sentiment classification. Currently, the attention mechanism is mainly combined with RNN (Recurrent Neural Network) or LSTM (Long Short-Term Memory) networks. Such neural network-based sentiment analysis model not only has a complicated computational structure, but also has computational dependence. To address the above problems and improve the accuracy of the target-based sentiment classification for short text, we propose a neural network model that combines deep-attention with Bidirectional Encoder Representations from Transformers (DA-BERT). The DA-BERT model can fully mine the relationships between target words and emotional words in a sentence, and it does not require syntactic analysis of sentences or external knowledge such as sentiment lexicon. The training speed of the proposed DA-BERT model has been greatly improved while removing the computational dependencies of RNN structure. Compared with LSTM, TD-LSTM, TC-LSTM, AT-LSTM, ATAE-LSTM, and PAT-LSTM, the results of experiments on the dataset SemEval2014 Task4 show that the accuracy of the DA-BERT model is improved by 13.63% on average where the word vector is 300 dimensions in aspect sentiment classification.

Keywords: Aspect sentiment classification · BERT · Deep-attention · Multi-attention · Part-of-speech · Sentiment analysis · Short text

1 Introduction

In recent years, the amount of addressing comments, opinions, and feelings on social media (e.g. Twitter, Wechat, Facebook, Weibo, Instagram, etc.) is greatly increased. Mining emotional sentiment in text from social media could yield huge commercial and social value. The use of natural language processing techniques for text sentiment analysis has become a hot topic of studying globally [1]. The sentiment analysis, also known as the opinion mining, is the basic task of NLP (Natural Language Processing)

© Springer Nature Switzerland AG 2019
P.-C. Yew et al. (Eds.): APPT 2019, LNCS 11719, pp. 86–95, 2019.
https://doi.org/10.1007/978-3-030-29611-7_7

domain and computational linguistics. Text information mining has received increasing attention in industry and academia recently. The deep learning model perform well in many natural language processing tasks, such as machine translation, semantic recognition, and text summaries. LSTM has achieved a great success in various NLP tasks. Yang et al. proposed two neural networks to model sentences and documents, first adopt CNN/LSTM to model sentence representations, and then using a Bi-GRU network model to encode sentence representations for document representation [2]. Bhatia et al. proposes a recursive neural network based on the RST structure to improve the classification accuracy of the text sentiment [3]. Today, many extended structure LSTMs are utilized for text sentiment classification. Tai et al. advocated a Tree-LSTM network model that achieved good results in predicting text sentiment classification [4]. Zhu et al. proposed an extended tree structure of LSTM, using semantic combination model to understand the meaning of text [5]. The attention mechanism was firstly proposed in the field of computer vision and digital images. Bahdanau et al. combined attention mechanisms and neural networks in machine translation [6]. The process of machine translation uses codec to simultaneously translate and align text-processing tasks. This is the first time researchers have tried to introduce attention mechanisms into the field of NLP, and it is proved the effectiveness of the combination of attention mechanisms and deep learning models. The attention mechanism can concentrate on different parts of a sentence when different aspects are taken as input. Neural attention can improve the ability to read comprehension. Wang et al. proposed attention-based Long Short-Term memory for aspect-level sentiment classification [7]. The models are able to attend different parts of a sentence when different aspects are concerned. Results show that the attention mechanism is effective. We put forward a classification model orienting to aspect sentiment based on BERT. The model can excavate the relationships between target words and emotional words in a sentence.

The major contributions of this work are as follows:

1. We put forward a novel network model (DA-BERT) that combines deep-attention with Bidirectional Encoder Representations from Transformers to solve the aspect-level sentiment analysis problem.
2. The DA-BERT model utilizes the part-of-speech of text information.
3. DA-BERT model gains higher accuracy of the sentiment classification than that of others.

The rest of this paper is structured as follows: Sect. 2 discusses the related works, Sect. 3 describe the DA-BERT model in detail, Sect. 4 presents extensive experiments to verify the effectiveness and performance of DA-BERT, and Sect. 5 summarizes our work and look into the future research.

2 Related Work

In this section, we will review related works on aspect-level sentiment classification and transformer theory.

2.1 Aspect Sentiment Classification

Different from the general sentiment analysis, the aspect-level sentiment classification aims to infer the sentiment polarity of a sentence depending not only on the context but also on the aspect [8]. We take a sentence as an example, "The service at that cafe was dreadful, but the cake tastes very good.". We can observe that, for aspect "cake", the sentiment polarity is positive while the sentiment polarity of aspect "service" is negative. Even in the same sentence, sentiment polarity could be absolutely opposite when focusing on different aspects. Wang et al. propose a new method to combine the syntactic structure and convolutional neural nets to directly match aspects and corresponding polarities [9].

The deep learning technology has made a significate breakthrough in text classification tasks. Many researchers used deep learning techniques to solve aspect-level sentiment analysis problems. TC-LSTM and TD-LSTM [10], which consider the aspect information, improve the accuracy of classification in sentiment analysis tasks for aspect-level. Introducing the attention mechanism in the classification model is an effective way to improve the accuracy of the level-level sentiment classification. Attention mechanism can fully explore the relationships between target words and emotional words in a sentence. AT-LSTM model and ATAE-LSTM model [7] model introduces an attention mechanism to capture the importance of different contextual information for a given aspect.

2.2 Transformer

Many natural language processing tasks can be regarded as sequence-to-sequence problem. The encoder-decoder model consisting of the traditional neural network model and has two inevitable defects in the processing of sequence problems: information loss problem and computational dependence.

In terms of the text feature extraction, transformer [11] as a feature extraction model is better than deep learning model in computational speed and information mining. The core idea of the Transformer framework is to calculate the relationship of each word in a sentence to all other words in the sentence. The relationship between these words and words reflects to some extent the relevance and importance of different words in this sentence. By using these interrelationships to adjust the weight of each word, a new embedding for each word can be obtained. This new embedding not only implies the word itself, but also contains the relationship between other words and the word, so it is a more global expression than the simple word vector. Transformer obtains the final textual representation by continuously overlaying the input text with such a layer of attention mechanism and a common nonlinear layer. We utilize the BERT model based on transformer encoder to extract text semantic, and propose a DA-BERT analysis model for text sentiment based on Bert's multi-attention mechanism.

3 BERT Model with Deep Attention

3.1 Bidirectional Encoder Representations from Transformers

Text feature extraction in the field of classifying text sentiment can be defined as a sequence problem. The encoder-decoder is a common sequence model framework for deep learning. Encoder is to convert the input sequence into a fixed-length vector. The decoder converts the vector generated by the encoder into the target sequence vector. Currently, optional encoders include CNN, LSTM, GRU, etc. These can also be used for decoders. Unsupervised algorithm automatic coding [12] is a typical encoder decoder model; the image caption for image is the encoder-decoder framework of CNN-RNN; the neural network machine translation model NMT [13] is an LSTM-LSTM encoder-decoder framework.

Although an encoder-decoder model consisting of a traditional neural network model which is widely used to handle sequence problems. However, there are two inevitable shortcoming of encoder-decoder model. First, the encoder transforms the input sequence into a vector of fixed length resulting in the loss of information. Second, because of the computational dependency problem of the sequence model, parallel computing cannot be implemented. Transformer [11] model alleviates the shortcomings of the sequence problem to a certain extent. The BERT can be thought of an encoder stack consisting of transformer.

Each encoder consists of a Feed Forward layer and a Multi-Head Attention layer. The input to the model continually flows to the upper layer of the encoder stack. The input of each layer is calculated by the self-attention layer and the feedforward network, then is passed to the next encoder.

The calculation formula of attention in encoder is as follows:

$$\text{Attention}(Q, K, V) = \text{softmax}\left(\frac{QK^T}{\sqrt{d_k}}\right)V \tag{1}$$

Q, K, V are abstract vectors for assisting attention calculation. Different vectors are obtained by multiplying the word vector X by three different weight matrices WQ, WK, WV. WQ, WK, and WV are suitable parameters learned from the model training process. The multi-head attention final output:

$$\text{head}_i = \text{Attention}\left(QW_i^Q, KW_i^K, VW_i^V\right) \tag{2}$$

$$\text{MultiHead}(Q, K, V) = \text{Concat}(\text{head}_1, \ldots, \text{head}_h)W^O \tag{3}$$

The output of multi-head attention enters the forward neural network layer:

$$\text{FFN}(x) = \max(0, \text{MultiHead}(Q, K, V)W_1 + b_1)W_2 + b_2 \tag{4}$$

W_1, W_2, b_1, b_2, are parameters for the model training process.

3.2 Deep Attention-Based BERT (DA-BERT)

In order to extract more emotional information about specific domain topics in textual information, we have proposed the Deep Attention-based BERT (DA-BERT) which is a peek-based multi-attention BERT. The improved model combines the part-of-speech information and the BERT model, in order to extract the aspect information, part-of-speech information and potential semantic information in the text. DA-BERT model mainly includes a coding layer, a feature fusion layer, and a pooling layer. The pooling layer retains the main fusion features while reducing the computational complexity of the model and preventing overfitting.

The output of the encoder structure in the model is $MF_i, h_{ci}, h_{ai}, h_{pi}$ respectively represent text semantic features, aspect information features and text part-of-speech features.

$$MF_i = MultiFeature(h_{ci}, h_{ai}, h_{pi}) = Concat(h_{ci}, h_{ai}, h_{pi}) \qquad (5)$$

Wt, bt are parameters for the model training process. a_i represents the attention weight of each word in the text (Fig. 1):

$$a_i = W^t MF_i + b^t, \sum_{i=1}^{n} a_i = 1 \qquad (6)$$

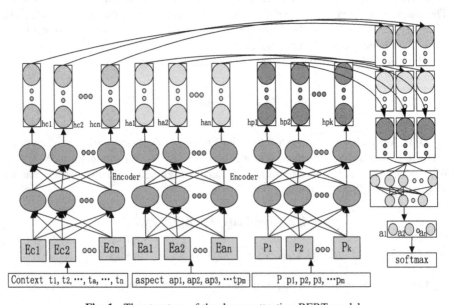

Fig. 1. The structure of the deeper-attention BERT model

h* as a feature of sentiment classification, the softmax classifier is used to classify texts.

$$h^* = \sum_{i=1}^{n} a_i \, MF_i \tag{7}$$

$$p = \text{softmax}(W_{MF}h^* + b_h) \tag{8}$$

The model proposed in this paper is trained by end-to-end back propagation, and the target loss function is cross entropy loss. Let y be the target distribution for sentence, y' be the predicted sentiment distribution. The goal of training is to minimize the cross-entropy error between y and y' for all sentences.

$$\text{loss} = -\sum_i \sum_j y_i^j \log y_i'^j + \lambda \|\theta\|^2 \tag{9}$$

Where i is the index of sentence, j is the index of aspect. Our classification is three ways. λ is the L2 - regularization term. θ is the parameter set.

4   Evaluation and Analysis

We apply the proposed model DA-BERT to aspect-level sentiment classification. The experimental test system is configured as Intel Core i7-8700K, GeForce RTX-2080Ti GPU, 3.9 TB Disk, and the operating system environment is Ubuntu 16.04-LTS-x86_64. The dimension of word vectors, aspect embedding and the text part-of-speech vector are consistent.

4.1   Dataset

We experiment on the dataset of SemEval 2014 Task 4 [7]. The dataset consists of both the Laptop and Restaurant themes. Since the comment text in the Laptop dataset does not include the domain-specific topic tags and the corresponding sentiment polarity classification, the Restaurant dataset is applied in this article. The data set retains text with positive, negative, and neutral emotion labels. The goal of the experiment is to extract corresponding emotional tendencies for different target words. The Restaurant dataset, which includes five domain-specific, are shown in Table 1.

Table 1. The restaurant dataset.

Target	Positive		Negative		Neural	
	Train	Test	Train	Test	Train	Test
Food	934	319	337	67	183	89
Price	261	63	162	29	26	16
Service	468	103	271	69	48	25
Ambience	298	74	105	18	51	23
Miscellaneous	711	133	247	27	410	79
Total	2672	692	1122	210	718	232

4.2 Baseline Models

We compared the DA-BERT model with several baselines, including LSTM [14], TD-LSTM, TC-LSTM, AT-LSTM, ATAE-LSTM, and PAT-LSTM [15]. LSTM takes the hidden state of the last word of the sentence as the input of the softmax classifier, and gets the emotional tendency of the whole sentence.TD-LSTM and TC-LSTM adds the aspect information when constructing the vector representation of the sentence.AT-LSTM, ATAE-LSTM introduces the attention mechanism to capture the importance of different context information to the aspect. PAT-LSTM can explore the relationships between target words and emotional words in a sentence.

4.3 Experimental Results Analysis

The DA-BERT model discards the traditional RNN network structure and uses the coding structure of the transformer to extract the semantic features of the text. In semantic extraction, the length of the calculation path between words in the self-attention [11] structure is $O(1)$, the computational complexity of each layer is $O(n^2d)$, and the length of the sequence calculation is $O(1)$; RNN performs information extraction. The maximum path length is $O(n)$, the computational complexity of each layer is $O(nd^2)$, and the sequence calculation length is $O(n)$; where d is the word vector dimension and n is the length of the sentence. As shown in Table 2, the computational complexity of self-attention is lower than that of RNN.

Table 2. Computational complexity

Layer type	Complexity	Sequential operations	Maximum path length
Self-attention	$O(n^2d)$	$O(1)$	$O(1)$
RNN	$O(nd^2)$	$O(n)$	$O(n)$

Table 3 shows the time takes for different models to complete an iteration where the text vector is 300 dimensions. It represents that the network training time cost of PAT-LSTM is relatively high, because of the sequence calculation properties of the LSTM model. The calculation of the information of t depends on the calculation result at $t - 1$. In this case, model parallelism cannot be achieved, and each hidden unit requires a series of complicated operations. When the text vector dimension is 300, the LSTM network model completes an iteration for about 510 s. The TD-LTM model adds aspect information while constructing the vector representation of the sentence, and the time to complete an iteration is about 30 s which is longer than that of LSTM model. The ATAE-LSTM model captures the importance of different contextual information for a given aspect through the attention mechanism, and combines the attention mechanism with LSTM to semantically model sentences. The addition of attention mechanism improves the computational complexity of the model and the training time of the model. The ATAE-LSTM model completed an iteration for about 40 s longer than the training time of the TD-LSTM model. The Bert-based multi-attention mechanism text sentiment classification model DA-BERT model proposed in this paper discards the information dependence of the RNN model and implements parallel computing. DA-BERT model takes about 19 s to complete an iteration, which is 30 times faster than the classification model that relies on the LSTM structure, effectively reducing the training time of the text classification model.

Table 3. Training time list of compared models

Model	Average time cost/s
PAT-LSTM	604
ATAE-LSTM	581
AT-LSTM	574
TC-LSTM	543
TD-LSTM	539
LSTM	512
DA-BERT	19

Table 4 that the classification effect of the DA-BERT model proposed in this paper is better than other models. When the word dimension is 300, the LSTM model achieves the best classification accuracy of 0.72. The standard LSTM cannot detect which is the important part for aspect-level sentiment classification. TD-LSMT constructs a sentence vector representation that considers not only the target word, but also the connection between the target vector and each context word. The classification accuracy of the TD-LSTM and TC-LSTM models is 0.05 and 0.08 higher than the LSTM model. TD-LSTM and TC-LSTM, which considered target information, achieved state-of-the-art performance in aspect sentiment classification. TC-LSTM obtained a target vector by averaging the vectors of words that the target phrase contains. However, simply averaging the word embedding of a target phrase is not sufficient to represent the semantics of the target phrase, resulting a suboptimal performance. The ATAE-LSTM model uses the attention mechanism to mine the importance of contextual information in a text for a given aspect. The ATAE-LSTM model has a classification accuracy of 0.84 on the dataset. The PAT-LSTM model can fully explore the relationships between target words and emotional words in a sentence. The classification accuracy of PAT-LSTM model for text sentiment is 0.06 higher than that of the AEAT-LSTM model. DA-BERT model combined with multiple attention mechanisms can make the model mine the emotional information of specific targets through the multi-attention mechanism in the process of training, and compensates for the shortcomings of the single attention mechanism, thus obtaining better classification effect. The classification accuracy rate of DA-BERT model for text sentiment reached 0.92.

Table 4. Classification accuracy list of compared models.

Dimension	50	100	150	200	250	300
LSTM	0.65857	0.68469	0.70705	0.71273	0.71201	0.72483
TC-LSTM	0.73136	0.75473	0.75853	0.76106	0.76966	0.77966
TD-LSTM	0.77445	0.78288	0.78917	0.79120	0.79308	0.81227
AT-LSTM	0.81114	0.81726	0.81907	0.82837	0.83613	0.83188
ATAE-LSTM	0.83267	0.83861	0.84347	0.84968	0.85319	0.84116
PAT-LSTM	0.86733	0.86925	0.87266	0.88798	0.90591	0.89154
DA-BERT	0.89685	0.89975	0.90356	0.90955	0.91556	0.92058

5 Conclusions

This paper proposes an analysis model DA-BERT for text sentiment based on Transformer encoder to extract text semantic. The model extracts semantic features and topic features from the input text and combines the part-of-speech features of the text as the target of the classification. Moreover, the DA-BERT model discards the RNN computational dependency structure, which enables parallel computing and shortens the model training time.

However, for text-level sentiment analysis tasks, the computational complexity of the attention value in the encoder increases dramatically which would result in slowing down the model. In the future, we would improve the performance of computing attention mechanism between words and words from the perspective of mathematical principles.

Acknowledgements. We would like to thank the anonymous reviewers for their invaluable comments. This work was partially funded by the Shanghai Pujiang Program under Grant 16PJ1407600, the China Post-Doctoral Science Foundation under Grant 2017M610230, and the National Natural Science Foundation of China under Grant 61332009, 61775139, and the Open Project Funding from the State Key Lab of Computer Architecture, ICT, CAS under Grant CARCH201807. Any opinions, findings and conclusions expressed in this paper are those of the authors and do not necessarily reflect the views of the sponsors.

References

1. Liu, B.: Sentiment analysis and opinion mining. Synth. Lect. Hum. Lang. Technol. **5**(1), 1–167 (2012)
2. Yang, Z., Yang, D., Dyer, C., He, X.: Hierarchical attention networks for document classification. In: Proceedings of the North American Chapter of the Association for Computational Linguistics: Human Language Technologies, pp. 1480–1489 (2017)
3. Bhatia, P., Ji, Y., Eisenstein, J.: Better document-level sentiment analysis from RST discourse parsing. Comput. Sci. 2212–2218 (2015)
4. Tai, K.S., Socher, R., Manning, C.D.: Improved semantic representations from tree-structured long short-term memory networks. In: Proceedings of the 53rd Annual Meeting of the Association for Computational Linguistic and the 7th International Joint Conference on Natural Language Processing, pp. 1556–1566 (2015)

5. Zhu, X., Sobhani, P., Guo, H.: Long short-term memory over tree structures. In: Proceedings of the 32nd International Conference on Machine Learning, 1604–1612 (2015)

6. Bahdanau, D., Cho, K., Bengio, Y.: Neural machine translation by jointly learning to align and translate. In: Proceedings of International Conference on Learning Representations, pp. 940–1000 (2015)

7. Wang, Y., Huang, M., Zhao, L., Zhu, X.: Attention-based LSTM for aspect-level sentiment classification. In: Proceedings of Conference on Empirical Methods in Natural Language Processing, pp. 606–615 (2016)

8. Dohaiha, H.H., Prasad, P.W.C., Maag, A., Alsadoon, A.: Deep learning for aspect-based sentiment analysis: a comparative review. Expert Syst. Appl. **118**, 272–299 (2019)

9. Wang, B., Liu, M.: Deep learning for aspect-based sentiment analysis [RT]. Stanford University report (2015). http://cs224d.stanford.edu/reports/WangBo.pdf

10. Tang, D., Qin, B., Feng, X.: Effective LSTMs for target-dependent sentiment classification. In: Proceedings of COLINE 2016, the 26th International Conference on Computational Linguistics: Technical Papers, pp. 3298–3307 (2016)

11. Vaswani, A., et al.: Attention is all you need. In: Advances in Neural Information Processing Systems, pp. 5998–6008 (2017)

12. Kingma, D.P., Welling, M.: Auto-encoding variational bayes. arXiv preprint arXiv:1312. 6114 (2013)

13. Sutskever, I., Vinyals, O., Le, Q.V.: Sequence to sequence learning with neural networks. In: Proceedings of the 27th International Conference on Neural Information Processing Systems, pp. 3104–3112 (2014)

14. Hochreiter, S., Schmidhuber, J.: Long short-term memory. Neural Comput. **9**(8), 1735–1780 (1997)

15. Pei, S., Wang, L.: Study on text sentiment analysis using attention mechanism. Comput. Eng. Sci. **2**, 343–354 (2019). (in Chinese)

16. Lin, Z., et al.: A structured self-attentive sentence embedding. arXiv preprint arXiv:1703. 03130 (2017)

Random Inception Module
and Its Parallel Implementation

Yingqi Gao, Kunpeng Xie, Song Guo, Kai Wang, Hong Kang, and Tao Li[✉]

College of Computer Science, Nankai University, Tianjin, China
{gaoyingqi,xkp,guosong}@mail.nankai.edu.cn,
{wangk,kanghong,litao}@nankai.edu.cn

Abstract. Inception module is proposed in GoogLeNet, which improves performance by increasing the width of the network. Multiple branches are computed in parallel, which makes the inception module naturally take the advantage of GPU high-performance computing. In this paper, we propose a parallel implementation of the inception module to accelerate the training and test of the inception networks. However, convolution neural networks are prone to overfitting due to the huge amount of parameters. We propose random inception module to avoid overfitting and accelerate inception module. In order to demonstrate the effectiveness of the proposed methods, we compare the performance of the random inception module with original inception module on CIFAR-10 dataset. Experimental results show our parallel inception module obtains over 2.8× speedup compared with Caffe. And our proposed RIM indeed behaves in a manner of regularization and speeds up convergence.

Keywords: CNN · Parallel computing · Inception module · Random drop

1 Introduction

In recent years, convolutional neural networks (CNN) have brought about a series of breakthroughs in the field of computer vision [7,8,10,12,14]. Unlike conventional machine learning methods, CNN automatically extract the most representative features. CNN typically have multiple convolution (followed by nonlinear activation) and pooling layers stacked, followed by several fully connected layers for classification. Back-propagation algorithm [11] is used for CNN training.

Since Krizhevsky et al. won ILSVRC competition in 2012 [10], a lot of efforts have been made to improve performance. VGG proposed by Simonyan et al. reduced the ILSVRC classification top-5 test error to 6.8% by pushing the depth to 16–19 weight layers [12]. Their experiments have shown that as the depth of increases, the representation power of the network is stronger. However, deeper networks are more difficult to optimize and leads to degradation problem. He et al. introduced shortcut connections and proposed deep residual learning to

© Springer Nature Switzerland AG 2019
P.-C. Yew et al. (Eds.): APPT 2019, LNCS 11719, pp. 96–106, 2019.
https://doi.org/10.1007/978-3-030-29611-7_8

ease the training of CNN [7]. DenseNet connected each layer to every other layer in a feed-forward fashion, which alleviated the vanishing-gradient problem and encouraged feature reuse [8].

Different from the several networks mentioned above, GoogLeNet has inception modules stacked on top of each other, which increases both the depth and width of the networks [14]. Inception and its variants have been widely used for image classification and semantic segmentation, etc. Szegedy et al. won ILSVRC competition by ensembling 7 GoogLeNet models in 2014. In 2016, Gulshan et al. trained an Inception-v3 network to detect referable diabetic retinopathy. They reported a sensitivity of 97.5% and a specificity of 93.4% on the EyePACS-1 dataset [6]. Chen et al. applied Xception model into semantic segmentation and achieved the test set performance of 89% on PASCAL VOC 2012 [4].

In an inception module, multiple convolution or pooling operations of different scales are executed in parallel, and then all the features are concatenated together. There are several inception modules stacked upon each other in an inception-type network. As the depth of the network increases, a greater speedup will be achieved. Although deep learning frameworks such as caffe, use GPUs for acceleration, the branches in the inception module is executed serially. In this paper, we specially design a parallel acceleration method for inception module. In addition, CNN is prone to overfitting due to its large number of parameters. In order to prevent overfitting, we present random inception module as regularization. During training time, RIM randomly select a path and set its weights to zero. Due to the difference in execution time of each path, RIM can reduce the training time of network.

The main contributions of this paper include the following:

- We propose random inception module which can prevent overfitting as a regularization and speed up the networks.
- We propose a parallel implementation of the inception module, which greatly shortens the training and testing time.
- We run experiments on CIFAR-10 dataset and results demonstrate the effectiveness of proposed methods.

The remainder of this paper is organized as follows. Section 2 provides a detailed description of the proposed method. Experimental settings and results are described in Sect. 3. The conclusion is drawn in Sect. 4.

2   Methods

In this section, we will introduce the architecture of the typical inception module and its parallel implementation. In addition, random inception module is introduced to avoid overfitting and accelerate the network.

2.1   Inception Module

Inception module is firstly introduced in GoogLeNet and derived many variants. The typical inception module has four parallel branches, as shown in Fig. 1(a).

For an input image, inception module performs multiple convolution operations or pooling operations in parallel. Then their outputs are concatenated into a single output vector. Different filter sizes, such as 1×1, 3×3, and 5×5 capture local information at different scales. Since pooling operations can extract features to a certain extent, a parallel pooling path is added. In order to reduce the computational complexity, 1×1 convolutions are used to reduce dimensionality. In addition, adding extra convolution layers means introducing more nonlinear activations and richer features can be extracted. Finally, multi-scale feature fusion helps to improve the representation of the network and enhance the adaptability of the network to the scale. In the inception module, multiple branches are computed in parallel, without affecting each other. This architecture makes it naturally suitable for GPU acceleration. In a typical inception-type network, there are several inception modules stacked upon each other, which leads to greater speedup.

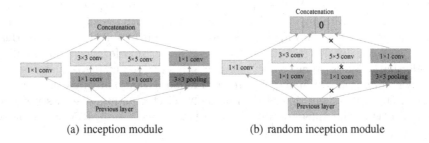

(a) inception module   (b) random inception module

Fig. 1. Visualization of inception module and our proposed random inception module.

2.2   Random Inception Module

There is a large amount of redundancy in deep neural network, as a result, it is easy to overfitting and falls into local minima or plateaus during training. A common method to address this problem is through regularization, such as weight decay and dropout [13]. In this section, we present random inception module (RIM) to handle this problem. On one hand, RIM can be regarded as a regularization method. On the other hand, it can be treated as a method to accelerate inception module (IM) since the forward and backward speed of RIM is much faster than that of IM.

Description. During training, RIM randomly selects a certain number of convolution operations in inception module during each iteration, and unselected convolutions contribute zero to RIM, as can be seen in Fig. 1(b). In this manner, RIM works in a way like dropout and dropblock [5], but with much stronger regularization. Moreover, from the perspective of model ensemble, a RIM corresponds to multiple different networks. For example, if we only select one convolution in

RIM, four models obtained. This ensemble means much better robustness. In addition, during backward pass, unselected convolutions contribute zero to the gradients of previous layer. When it comes to inference phase, there is more than one way to give an output of RIM. One natural way is that we can consider all sub-models' output and vote for the final result. Or we can scale the weights in RIM by a constant value which is related to the number of convolutions retained.

Running Time Analysis. There are four groups of convolutions in inception module. And the forward time for each group of convolution is t_1, t_2, t_3 and t_4. Suppose each group convolution is selected with equal probability and we omit the concatenation time for simplicity.

For a serial implementation of inception module, the forward time during one iteration for IM and RIM are formulated as:

$$TS_{IM} = \sum_{i=1}^{4} t_i \tag{1}$$

$$E[TS_{RIM}(R)] = \frac{R}{4} \sum_{i=1}^{4} t_i \tag{2}$$

where R denotes the number of convolutions kept and $E[TS_{RIM}(R)]$ is the expected value of TS_{RIM}. Thus, the expected speedup of RIM is $\frac{4}{R}$. Specially, RIM can achieve a maximum speedup of four times compared with IM with the same number of iterations, if we only select one convolution out of inception.

As well, for a parallel implementation of inception module, the forward time during each iteration for IM and RIM are formulated as:

$$TP_{IM} = \max\{t_i | i = 1, 2, 3, 4\} \tag{3}$$

$$E[TP_{RIM}(R)] = \begin{cases} \frac{t_1 + t_2 + t_3 + t_4}{4}, & R = 1 \\ \frac{1}{2}t_{k_1} + \frac{1}{3}t_{k_2} + \frac{1}{6}t_{k_3}, & R = 2 \\ \frac{3}{4}t_{k_1} + \frac{1}{4}t_{k_2}, & R = 3 \\ t_{k_1} & R = 4 \end{cases} \tag{4}$$

where t_{k_i} denotes the ith largest value among $t_1, ..., t_4$. We can observe that the upper bound of the speedup is $4\times$ when R is set to 1.

2.3   Parallel Implementation

GPU Architecture. In this experiment, GeForce GTX1080Ti GPU based on Pascal architecture is used, and the core version is GP102-350. We provide a detailed introduction to the GP102 core of the Pascal architecture here.

NVIDIA GPU is built from a multi-threaded Streaming Multiprocessor (SM) array. GTX 1080Ti contains 28 SMs and each SM contains 128 CUDA cores. So

GTX 1080Ti is equipped with 3584 CUDA cores in total. In addition, each SM contains 32 SFUs (Special Function Units). SFU provides hardware acceleration for some special function instructions, including $\sin x$, $\cos x$, $\log x$, 2^x, $1/x$, et al. Each SM is equipped with 4 warp schedulers and 8 instruction distribution units. Each warp manages 32 cuda cores, which means that up to 4 warps can be executed in parallel in the same SM. Each warp scheduler is responsible for the scheduling of a warp and can be assigned two instructions per GPU cycle. Each SM is equipped with 256 KB of register file space, 96 KB of shared memory, and 48 KB of L1 cache, which provides higher bandwidth and lower latency than global memory.

Table 1 shows the configuration comparison of several different GPUs in the Pascal architecture. GTX 1080Ti has a huge improvement compared with GTX 1080. The number of SMs has increased by 8, which means GTX 1080Ti can execute more threads concurrently than GTX 1080. The number of SMs in the Tesla P100 is double that of the GTX 1080Ti, but the number of warps in a single SM is reduced by half, which is equivalent to reducing the size of the SM, but the number is increased. Each SM of Tesla P100 contains 64 single-precision floating-point CUDA cores and 32 double-precision floating-point CUDA cores, which are more powerful than GTX 1080Ti.

Table 1. GPU configuration comparison of pascal architecture.

	Core version	Transistor	SM number	Core/SM	Shared memory/SM	Warps/SM
GTX 1080Ti	GP102-350	12 billion	28	128	96 KB	4
GTX 1080	GP104-100	7.2 billion	20	128	96 KB	4
Tesla P100	GP100	15.3 billion	56	96	64 KB	2

Parallel Implementation. Training a deep neural network model usually takes hours or even longer. NVIDIA's GPU, equipped with a large number of cuda cores, provides powerful computing power and parallel computing resources, which can mitigate the time-consuming problems in deep learning. GPU mode has been successfully applied to several neural network frameworks, for example Caffe [9], TensorFlow [2] and Theano [3]. These deep learning systems only accelerate the calculation of each layer of the neural network using deep learning libraries such as cuda, cublas, and cudnn on GPU. For the inception layer, it is always a fusion of several independent groups. Each group contains one or more layers. By implementing parallel computing of inception, we can further accelerate the training of neural networks. Today's GPUs are not only capable of fast calculations for a single task, but also support multitasking parallelism within its computing resources. On GPU, different streams, execute their commands out of order with respect to one another or concurrently [1].

Figure 2 shows the parallel implementation framework for the inception layer. Each group of computational operations is merged into one stream. The operations between these streams are strictly independent. It is reasonable to employ this parallel model. Concat layer always follows the inception layer. It splices the output feature maps of all groups on the C channel or the N channel. During this splicing process, it contains a large number of fragmented memory copies. Using a simple assignment copy of multiple threads with GPU instead of multiple memory copies can significantly improve the performance of the program, like caffe. We propose a method of breaking up the concat layer, and then assigning them to each stream for execution. For example, after the calculation of *GROUP1* done, the assignment copy of the output of *GROUP1* can be done immediately.

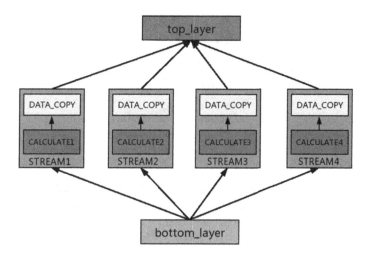

Fig. 2. Overview of parallel implementation of inception module.

3   Experiments

In order to demonstrate the effectiveness of the proposed methods, we ran experiments on CIFAR-10 dataset and evaluated its performance.

3.1   Baseline Model

Our baseline model is designed based on GoogLeNet where inception module is introduced. In our baseline model, only one inception module is used. All the convolutions are followed by ReLU activation function. The weights of convolution and fully connected layers are initialized with uniform distributions between -0.05 and 0.05. The overview of baseline is shown in Fig. 3.

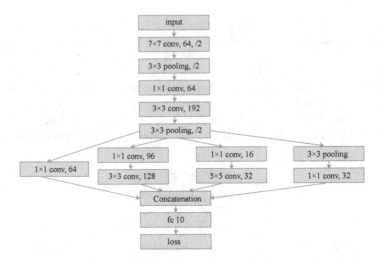

Fig. 3. An overview of baseline model.

3.2   Running Environments

We ran our networks on a workstation equipped with four Nvidia GeForce GTX 1080Ti GPUs, 128G RAM and the operating system is Ubuntu 16.04. We use CUDA and CUDNN to implement the baseline model and their versions are 8.0 and 6.0, respectively.

3.3   Results

We evaluate our methods on the CIFAR-10 dataset. CIFAR-10 consists of 60,000 colored natural images with 32×32 pixels, including 50,000 for training and 10,000 for test. We use all training images and report performance on the test images.

Running Time Analysis. First, we measure the running time of our implemented inception module, RIM and IM in Caffe when batch size is set to 50. We ran experiments on two networks, one with one IM (as shown in Fig. 3) and the other with two IMs. The number of convolutions in each IM is the same. Each experiments were repeated 100 times and the average forward and backward time are summarized in Table 2.

Table 2. Running time (μs) analysis of inception model.

Networks	Caffe (cudnn)		Parallel IM		RIM (R = 3)	
	Forward	Backward	Forward	Backward	Forward	Backward
baseline model (1 IM)	557.53	622.07	198.47	403.01	171.15	363.68
Baseline model (3 IM)	1774.15	1928.99	553.68	1186.93	484.14	1130.79

We can observe from Table 2 that our implemented parallel IM has a speedup 2.8× in forward time compared with Caffe. Moreover, the speedup can leads to 3.2× when random mechanism is introduced in parallel IM. When 3 IMs are embedded in the network, parallel IM has a speedup 3.2× in forward time compared with Caffe. And parallel RIM obtain a speedup 3.67×. In summary, as the number of incepeion modules in the network increases, the greater speedup can be obtained.

Random Inception Module. In this section, we compare the performance of IM and RIM. The running time of each epoch and the accuracy on the test set for IM and RIM are reported in Table 3. Compared with IM, there is no obvious loss of accuracy when R is 3. As the number of dropped branches increases, the loss of accuracy becomes more and more serious. In particular, the accuracy loss is about 9% when R is 1. The smaller the value of R, the less time each epoch runs. When we increase the depth of the network to three IMs, we obtain speedups of 1.08, 1.25 and 1.4375 when R is set to 3, 2 and 1 respectively compared with parallel IM. The accuracy increases by 2.17% when one IM is dropped. However, we fail to train the network when only one IM is remained and only get an accuracy of 22%. We guess this is caused by the small capacity of the network, the receptive field of 1×1 convolution is too small and the ability to extract features is very weak.

In addition, when one IM is embedded in the network, the curves of loss and accuracy against each epoch are shown in Fig. 4. For a learning rate of 0.01, the accuracy on the test set of IM begins to decline after training about 20 epochs. But the accuracy of RIM is slowly rising and gradually reaching a steady level. This indicates that our RIM has effectively prevented over-fitting. For a small learning rate of 0.001, when more convolutions are dropped, the loss reduces slowly since the capacity of the network is too small.

Table 3. Performance of IM and RIM.

Networks	Parallel IM		RIM (R = 3)			RIM (R = 2)			RIM (R = 1)		
	Time (s)	Acc (%)	Time (s)	Speedup	Acc (%)	Time (s)	Speedup	Acc (%)	Time (s)	Speedup	Acc (%)
Baseline model (1 IM)	1.8	64.02	1.72	1.04	63.08	1.64	1.10	61.81	1.60	1.125	55.11
Baseline model (3 IM)	2.99	62.17	2.68	1.08	**64.31**	2.39	1.25	60.98	2.08	1.4375	22

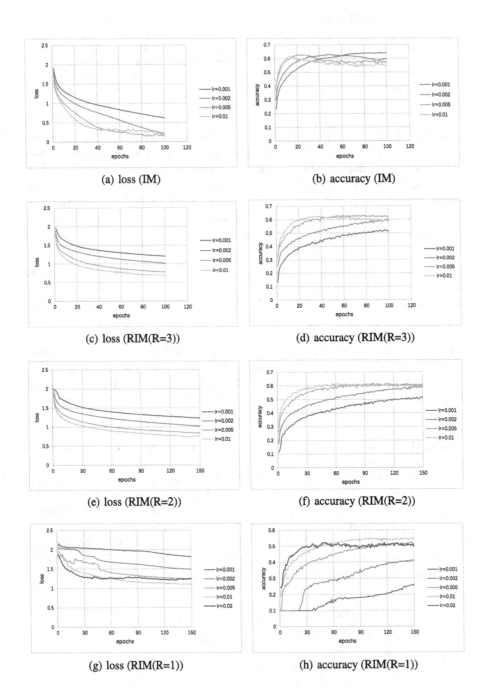

(a) loss (IM)

(b) accuracy (IM)

(c) loss (RIM(R=3))

(d) accuracy (RIM(R=3))

(e) loss (RIM(R=2))

(f) accuracy (RIM(R=2))

(g) loss (RIM(R=1))

(h) accuracy (RIM(R=1))

Fig. 4. Loss and accuracy of each epoch during training for IM and RIM with different parameter settings.

4 Conclusion

In this paper, we propose a parallel implementation of inception module, which leads to over 2.8× speedup compared with Caffe. In addition, we propose random inception module and experimental results show that it can effectively avoid overfitting and speed up convergence. In future, we plan to ensemble several networks with RIM. Since each network has a certain randomness, the results of multiple network voting will be better than a single network.

Acknowledgements. This work is partially supported by the National Natural Science Foundation (61872200), the National Key Research and Development Program of China (2016YFC0400709), the Science and Technology Commission of Tianjin Binhai New Area (BHXQKJXM-PT-ZJSHJ-2017005), the Natural Science Foundation of Tianjin (18YFYZCG00060) and Nankai University (91922299).

References

1. Cuda toolkit documentation v10.0.130. https://docs.nvidia.com/cuda
2. Abadi, M., et al.: Tensorflow: a system for large-scale machine learning, pp. 265–283 (2016)
3. Bergstra, J., et al.: Theano: A CPU and GPU math compiler in Python. In: Proceedings of the 9th Python in Science Conference, pp. 3–10 (2010)
4. Chen, L.-C., Zhu, Y., Papandreou, G., Schroff, F., Adam, H.: Encoder-decoder with atrous separable convolution for semantic image segmentation. In: Ferrari, V., Hebert, M., Sminchisescu, C., Weiss, Y. (eds.) ECCV 2018. LNCS, vol. 11211, pp. 833–851. Springer, Cham (2018). https://doi.org/10.1007/978-3-030-01234-2_49
5. Ghiasi, G., Lin, T., Le, Q.V.: Dropblock: a regularization method for convolutional networks. In: Neural Information Processing Systems, pp. 10750–10760 (2018)
6. Gulshan, V., et al.: Development and validation of a deep learning algorithm for detection of diabetic retinopathy in retinal fundus photographs. JAMA **316**(22), 2402–2410 (2016)
7. He, K., Zhang, X., Ren, S., Sun, J.: Deep residual learning for image recognition. In: Proceedings of the IEEE Conference on Computer Vision and Pattern Recognition, pp. 770–778 (2016)
8. Huang, G., Liu, Z., Van Der Maaten, L., Weinberger, K.Q.: Densely connected convolutional networks. In: Proceedings of the IEEE Conference on Computer Vision and Pattern Recognition, pp. 4700–4708 (2017)
9. Jia, Y., et al.: Caffe: convolutional architecture for fast feature embedding. CoRR abs/1408.5093 (2014). http://arxiv.org/abs/1408.5093
10. Krizhevsky, A., Sutskever, I., Hinton, G.E.: Imagenet classification with deep convolutional neural networks. In: Advances in Neural Information Processing Systems, pp. 1097–1105 (2012)
11. Rumelhart, D.E., Hinton, G.E., Williams, R.J., et al.: Learning representations by back-propagating errors. Cogn. Model. **5**(3), 1 (1988)
12. Simonyan, K., Zisserman, A.: Very deep convolutional networks for large-scale image recognition. In: International Conference on Learning Representations (2015)

13. Srivastava, N., Hinton, G., Krizhevsky, A., Sutskever, I., Salakhutdinov, R.: Dropout: a simple way to prevent neural networks from overfitting. J. Mach. Learn. Res. **15**(1), 1929–1958 (2014)
14. Szegedy, C., et al.: Going deeper with convolutions. In: The IEEE Conference on Computer Vision and Pattern Recognition (CVPR), June 2015

Security and Algorithms

CBA-Detector: An Accurate Detector Against Cache-Based Attacks Using HPCs and Pintools

Beilei Zheng$^{(\boxtimes)}$, Jianan Gu, and Chuliang Weng

School of Data Science and Engineering, East China Normal University,
Shanghai, China
{zhengbeilei,gjn}@stu.ecnu.edu.cn, clweng@dase.ecnu.edu.cn

Abstract. Cloud computing is convenient to provide adequate resources for tenants, but it suffers from information disclosure risks because hardware resources are shared among multiple tenants. For example, secret information in the shared cache can be inferred by other malicious processes, which is called cache-based attacks. To defeat against such attacks, many detection methods have been proposed. However, most of the existing detection mechanisms completely rely on the hardware performance counters (HPCs) and induce high false positives in detecting attacks. This paper proposes an accurate detector named CBA-Detector to detect cache-based side-channel attacks in real time. CBA-Detector is composed of an offline analysis phase and an online detection phase. The former analyzes the hardware events generated by sample programs. Then it extracts features from these events to train machine learning models. Based on the models, the latter monitors active processes in real time to discover suspicious processes. These suspicious processes will be checked again at the instruction level by customized Pintools, which effectively eliminates false positives. As shown in our experiments, CBA-Detector can accurately identify attacks in real time and introduces 4.4% overhead on PARSEC and about 10% overhead on web server.

Keywords: Cache-based side-channel attacks ·
Hardware performance counters · Pintools · False positives

1 Introduction

Cloud computing brings convenience to tenants, but it also faces enormous security risks. In the cloud, multiple tenants share hardware resources, and the shared processors can be abused by adversaries to mount micro-architectural attacks. These attacks result in a significant risk of information leakage in cloud platforms. For example, the recently discovered Meltdown [8] and Spectre [7] allow unauthorized processes to read data of privileged kernel or other processes.

One of the main micro-architecture attacks is the cache-based side-channel attack [5,10,17], through which an adversary can infer secret information of

© Springer Nature Switzerland AG 2019
P.-C. Yew et al. (Eds.): APPT 2019, LNCS 11719, pp. 109–122, 2019.
https://doi.org/10.1007/978-3-030-29611-7_9

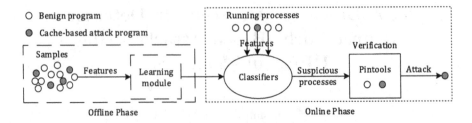

Fig. 1. The framework of CBA-Detector

a running process by observing the state of the shared cache. To carry out this attack, there are two requirements. On one hand, the adversary needs the ability to manipulate the shared cache to a specific state. On the other hand, the shared cache should have at least one distinguishable feature among different states. These two requirements become the key intuition to many existing studies against these attacks. For example, some defensive measures [4,6,9] devote to limiting the ability of the attackers to manipulate the shared cache, but many of them need to modify the operating system. Some detection efforts [1,11] against these attacks focus on observing some hardware events generated by programs through hardware performance counters (HPCs). They are inspired by the fact that intentional manipulation of the cache usually causes anomalous behaviors, such as high cache misses, which can be used for detecting these attacks.

However, many existing detection schemes completely rely on the data collected with HPCs, leading to high false-positive rates (benign programs are incorrectly identified as malicious) because the values collected with HPCs lack determinism [3]. For example, the false positives introduced by [1] and [11] are 0.1%–21.4% and 0–36.15%, respectively. Although [18] reduces the false positives by adjusting parameters, it is neither flexible nor thorough to solve this problem. Considering the high false positives, these methods are hardly deployed in real world.

To effectively detect attacks without false positives, we propose CBA-Detector. It can accurately identify cache-based side-channel attacks in real time, and it does not require modifying the operating system or the hardware. As shown in Fig. 1, CBA-Detector has two phases. During the offline phase, it first uses HPCs to collect hardware events of sample programs and analyzes these events through machine learning technologies to generate classifiers. Based on these classifiers, it determines suspicious programs during the online phase. Then it checks suspicious processes via customized Pintools, which can identify real attacks at the instruction level and eliminate false positives caused by classifiers.

Our main contributions are concluded as follows:

- We propose CBA-Detector, which combines hardware events with special instructions to detect cache-based side-channel attacks in real time. Besides, it gets rid of false positives in our experiments.
- We design and implement the prototype of CBA-Detector and show how it works in the offline phase and online phase.

– We evaluate CBA-Detector from three aspects, i.e., timeliness, accuracy and performance. As our experiments show, CBA-Detector can accurately detect cache-based side-channel attacks before they complete, and it only induces a little performance overhead.

The remainder of this paper is organized as follows. Section 2 contains the necessary background information on cache-based attacks, HPCs and Pintools. Section 3 defines the threat model and assumptions of this work. We describe the detailed design and implementation of CBA-Detector in Sect. 4. Section 5 evaluates and discusses CBA-Detector. Section 6 gives an overview of related work, and Sect. 7 concludes this paper.

2   Background

2.1   Cache-Based Attacks

Caches in modern processors are used for caching and retrieving frequently accessed instructions and data. Cached data usually costs less time to be accessed and more time to be flushed than the non-cached. This feature is abused by adversaries to mount cache-based side-channel attacks, such as Prime+Probe [10], Flush+Reload [17] and Flush+Flush [5]. The necessary procedure of these attacks is as follows: Firstly, the adversary manipulates the cache shared with the victim to a specific state. Then it waits for the victim to execute. After that, the adversary probes the time of loading/flushing specific addresses to infer the state of the shared cache, which may be changed during the execution of the victim. Therefore, the adversary can deduce from the state that which addresses have been accessed by the victim. As a result, the adversary can successfully infer the secret information of the victim.

Flush+Reload, Flush+Flush and Prime+Probe are three most well-known cache-based side-channel attacks. Flush+Reload and Flush+Flush employ the clflush instruction to manipulate the shared cache, while Prime+Probe evicts target data by accessing addresses mapped to the same cache set. The rdtsc or rdtscp instruction can be used for measuring the time of loading/flushing data from the shared cache, and they usually combine with lfence, mfence or cpuid instruction to obtain precise timestamps. Moreover, some cache-based attacks invoke the system call sched yield frequently to increase the chance of stealing data. These features are an important basis of detection.

2.2   Hardware Performance Counters (HPCs)

HPCs are a set of special-purpose registers directly provided by a dedicated unit of modern CPUs called a Performance Monitoring Unit (PMU). They store various CPU-related events such as cache hits/misses. Hardware events can help software vendors to enhance their code to improve performance by profiling the behavior of a program. Recently, HPCs have been also used for detecting cache-based attacks in the field of system security.

HPCs can be accessed with the command `perf` provided by Linux. One of the most common used sub-commands of `perf` is `perf-stat`, which can collect various pre-defined hardware events and software events on a system-wide, process and thread basis. However, the minimum sampling interval of `perf-stat` is 100 ms. Unlike `perf`, Performance Application Programming Interface (PAPI) [15] is another library that provides a consistent interface and methodology for us to use HPCs. It can sample hardware events in nearly real time with a minimum sampling interval of three microseconds [2].

2.3 Pintools

Pin is a dynamic binary instrumentation (DBI) framework developed by Intel [13] and allows us to customize dynamic program analysis tools, i.e., Pintools. Pintools are powerful because they do not require source code of a program and can insert arbitrary codes in any places in the executable programs to analyze program. Besides, the code is added dynamically while the executable program is running so that it is possible to attach Pintools to a running process.

3   Threat Model and Assumptions

We assume that the attackers have the ability to execute user-level codes on the system so that they can steal secret information via cache-based side-channel attacks. Prime+Probe [10], Flush+Reload [17] and Flush+Flush [5], as three most well-known cache-based side-channel attacks, are focused in this work. Specifically, we focus on these three attacks based on the last level cache (LLC) because LLC is shared among processor cores and easy to be attacked. Unless specified otherwise, all the attacks mentioned in this paper are LLC attacks. LLC attacks can extract secrets across multiple processor cores and across virtual machine boundaries. As a result, virtual machines and desktop computers are the targets of our protection.

The trusted computing base includes the underlying hardware, hypervisor and operating system. Thus, we trust that the data collected from HPCs would not be tampered by other processes and the operating system does not compromise to other attacks like return-oriented programming (ROP). We further assume CBA-Detector can run properly, and it cannot be disabled by attackers.

Based on the above assumptions, CBA-Detector can detect Prime+Probe, Flush+Reload and Flush+Flush attacks both in desktop computers and virtual machines in real time. Other attacks steal secrets with the help of these attacks can be detected as well, such as the recently discovered Spectre and Meltdown. Furthermore, CBA-Detector can also detect rowhammer because it uses `clflush` instruction at high frequency. However, some attacks run in SGX are out of the scope of this study because reliable performance counters are not available in SGX enclaves.

4 Design and Implementation

4.1 Overview

Figure 2 gives an overview of the architecture of CBA-Detector, which is composed of four modules, i.e., a monitoring module, a learning module, a detection module and a verification module. Overall, the design of CBA-Detector is divided into two phases: an offline phase and an online phase. During the offline phase, the offline monitor works with the learning module to generate classifiers for prediction. The classifiers can be migrated to different environments for real-time detection. In the online phase, the online monitor collects events and sends real-time data of events to the detection module, which determines suspicious processes according to the prediction of classifiers. Suspicious processes will be checked by customized Pintools in the verification module to eliminate false positives and identify real attacks. The four modules are designed as follows:

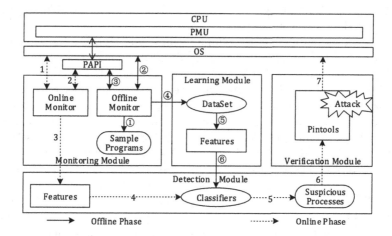

Fig. 2. Overview of CBA-Detector

Monitoring Module is composed of an offline monitor and an online monitor. The former collects hardware events of sample programs and saves these data for later analysis, while the latter collects events of running processes in the system and sends the collected data to the detection module in real time.

Learning Module attempts to train classifiers that can make predictions with high accuracy. To achieve this goal, the collected data is split into windows and suitable features are extracted from each window to train machine learning models. Then the generated classifiers are saved for real-time detection.

Detection Module is expected to detect all possible malicious processes in real time. To satisfy this expectation, the real-time data from the online monitor is divided into windows with fixed size. In each window, features are figured out and fed to classifiers to predict whether potential attacks exist or not. If the prediction of the classifiers turns out positive, the CBA-Detector concludes that the corresponding process of the window is a suspicious process. Then the verification module is launched to check the suspicious process at the instruction level with customized Pintools.

Verification Module aims at eliminating misjudgments of classifiers and identifying real attacks from the suspicious processes. Here, the customized Pintools will attach to the suspicious processes to identify attacks at the instruction level. Once a real attack is found, CBA-Detector will report it to the operating system.

Next, we will provide the detailed implementation of CBA-Detector.

4.2   The Offline Phase

The offline phase prepares classifiers for the online phase. As shown in Fig. 2, it involves the monitoring module and the learning module. The former collects hardware events of sample processes, while the latter trains classifiers based on the collected data of events.

In the monitoring module, the offline monitor first launches the sample programs (step ①), then gets the process id (pid) of the launched program from the operating system (step ②). The sample programs include attacks and benign programs. Specifically, the attacks are composed of Prime+Probe, Flush+Reload and Flush+Flush. To the best of our knowledge, the core code of these attacks is a loop structure, which is the main detecting target of CBA-Detector. Since some compute-intensive programs contain many loop structures as well, we select the applications of SPECCPU 2006 benchmark as benign sample programs. Then the offline monitor collects events of the process whose pid equals to the specific pid (step ③). To obtain hardware events, we use interfaces provided by PAPI to access PMU. Hardware events to be monitored include total cycles, total instructions, total LLC cache accesses and LLC load misses, which are selected based on the experience of existing works [11,18]. Finally, the offline monitor writes the collected data to files (step ④).

In the learning module, the data collected by the offline monitor is analyzed, and suitable features are extracted (step ⑤). As mentioned above, the offline monitor collects four hardware events (a.k.a. an event vector) every three microseconds. Since the core code for attacking is usually a loop structure, we extract the events of loops for attacking and consider the set of event vectors of each loop as a window. Similarly, we split the event vectors of benign programs into fixed size windows. In each window, we build a feature vector. Specifically, we first compute six values from each event vector, i.e., the cache miss rate, instruction per cycle, load misses per cycle, cache accesses per cycle, load misses per instruction and cache accesses per instruction. For each value, we extract six attributes (i.e., the average, standard deviation, minimum, lower quartile, upper quartile and maximum) from event vectors in a window as a feature vector, whose dimension of is 36. These feature vectors are labeled and divided into two classes, i.e., attacks and benign windows. We call the labeled feature vectors record, which will be fed to three common and quite different machine learning learners (step ⑥), i.e., Multilayer Perceptron (mlp), CART Decision tree (dec), and XGBoost (xgb). Then we use the K-fold cross-validation technique to select the best model, where K is five here. Specifically, we first take 30% attack records as the testing set and the rest 70% of them as the training set. Since there are far more benign records (370935) than attacks (37066) in the dataset, we choose the undersampling technique to get 10% benign records as the training set and the rest as the testing set. Then the training set is randomly divided into five parts, among which four are used as the training set, while the rest one is used as the verification set. After five repetitions, the model with the minimum verification errors is saved for real-time detection.

4.3   The Online Phase

Based on the classifiers generated during the offline phase, the online phase detects active processes in real time. This phase involves the monitoring module, the detection module and the verification module. The monitoring module collects real-time events of active processes in the system, then the detection module determines all possible attacks with the classifiers according to the collected data, finally the verification module checks suspicious processes through customized Pintools at the instruction level to eliminate false positives.

The online monitor in the monitoring module has a similar function to the offline monitor, but it watches the active processes in the system rather than sample programs. In detail, the online monitor has three key duties. First, it continually reads the /proc directory to get pids of running processes (step 1). Second, it watches the processes according to the pids for obtaining hardware events (step 2). Meanwhile, it counts the number of the system call sched yield in processes via perf. Third, the collected real-time data is transmitted in the form of stream data to the detection module (step 3).

In the detection module, the real-time data is divided into windows with fixed size and features are figured out in each window (step 3). Then these feature vectors are fed to classifiers for prediction (step 4). If a feature vector of a window is judged as anomalous by the classifiers, the corresponding process of which will be considered as a suspicious process (step 5). To eliminate misjudgments of the classifiers, the verification module will be launched to check suspicious processes on the instruction level (step 6).

The verification module aims at eliminating the false positives of classifiers. It checks suspicious processes at the instruction level via customized Pintools to identify real attacks. The Pintools count the number of clflush, rdtsc, rdtscp, cpuid, mfench and lfench instructions to determine attacks. These instructions are frequently used by three types of attacks, so the Pintools can accurately identify attacks. However, Pintools can only attach to processes whose user is the same as its own user. Therefore, CBA-Detector first executes the command runuser to login with the user of the suspicious process, then the Pintools can successfully attach to the process and count special instructions. If the Pintools regards a suspicious process as an attack, CBA-Detector will report the process

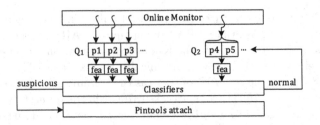

Fig. 3. The workflow of real-time detection

to the operating system (step 7). Although customized Pintools can effectively identify attacks, we still build classifiers at the first place. It is because the Pintools need to insert codes for counting special instructions at runtime, which will increase the execution time of programs and affect some applications that require precise timings. Therefore, we first use classifiers to filter out most of the benign processes to minimize the negative impact on benign programs.

4.4   Optimizations

In theory, the online monitor is necessary to watch all active processes in the system to avoid missing any possible attack. However, there are many active processes in the system and most of them are benign. In fact, there is no need to monitor programs that are sure to be benign. So how to efficiently monitor the running processes without missing any potential attack?

To solve this problem, we use an incremental monitoring approach. CBA-Detector continually takes a snapshot of pids of all running processes in the system at a regular interval and compares every two successive snapshots to find newborn processes, which are monitored by the online monitor. It can significantly reduce the number of processes that need to be monitored. Besides, we set up a whitelist to further reduce the number of processes to be monitored. We do not monitor a process if its pid or its parent pid (ppid) is in the whitelist. In our experiments, we only add the pid of kthreadd process (which is the parent of kernel processes) and the pid of CBA-Detector to the whitelist.

In this way, CBA-Detector just needs to monitor few newborn processes. However, when a monitored process is a service that needs a long time to run, the cost will be non-negligible if we keep monitoring the process throughout its lifetime. Thus, we adopt different strategies to monitor different processes, i.e., monitoring short-lived processes throughout their lifetime and watching long-lived processes in stages.

To distinguish different processes, CBA-Detector maintains two queues: a filter queue (Q_1) and a long-lived program queue (Q_2). Q_1 holds pids of new processes except some processes whose pid or ppid is in the whitelist. The online monitor continuously watches the new processes for several windows. If an abnormality is detected within these windows, the corresponding process will be labeled as suspicious. The suspicious process will be checked by the customized

Pintools at the instruction level. If a process does not complete within these windows, and no abnormal behavior is detected, CBA-Detector will move its pid to Q_2. Since there is no abnormality detected at the beginning, the online monitor appropriately relaxes detection, i.e., it watches these processes in turn. The procedure of the prediction of classifiers in Q_2 is the same as Q_1.

Figure 3 shows the workflow of the real-time detector. To avoid missing potential attacks, the online monitor creates a thread for each process in Q_1 to collect events. For some programs with a long lifetime, the online monitor creates a thread for all processes in Q_2 to collect events in turn. This way can save resources and reduce costs when there are some long-lived processes need to be monitored in the system. Thanks to the incremental monitoring method and the whitelist, only a few processes are monitored at a time. Thus, processes in queues are monitored in high density, and attacks can hardly evade the detection. Thus, CBA-Detector can efficiently monitor processes without missing any attack.

5   Evaluation

In this section, we evaluate CBA-Detector from three aspects: *timeliness, accuracy,* and *performance*. All experiments try to answer the following questions.

- *Q-1*: Can CBA-Detector detect attacks before they complete? (*timeliness*)
- *Q-2*: Does CBA-Detector eliminate false positives? (*accuracy*)
- *Q-3*: How much overhead does CBA-Detector introduce? (*performance*)

We evaluate the CBA-Detector on an x86-64 machine and a virtual machine (VM). The x86-64 machine has a 4-core Intel Core i5-4460 with 3.2 GHz clock frequency and 8 GB RAM. The VM is equipped with 2 vCPUs and 1 GB RAM. The operating system used in both environments is Centos 7.5.1804 with kernel Linux 3.10.0.

5.1   Real-Time Detection

To answer *Q-1*, we implement three PoCs (proof of concepts) of Spectre attack to steal 1024 bytes secret information through Prime+Probe, Flush+Reload and Flush+Flush, respectively. We run these attacks 10 times and compute the average ratio between the time to detect an attack and the time it needs to complete. Figure 4 depicts the results of the three implementations in different workloads, where the legend "Host 30%" refers that the CPU utilization of the host is 30%. We execute several firefox and gedit processes to set up different workloads and run live videos on Youtube to contend memory.

As shown in Fig. 4, all the three implementations of Spectre can be detected in real time both in the Host and VM, and there is no false negatives (malicious processes are incorrectly identified as benign) in our experiments. The detection of spectre_ff (spectre with Flush+Flush) is the fastest because it uses the `clflush` instruction with the highest frequency. The detection time in the VM

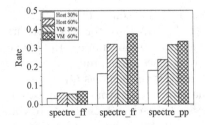

Fig. 4. Timeliness evaluation

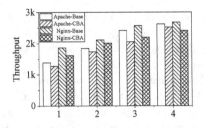

Fig. 5. Performance on web servers

is longer than that in the host because the number of cores of the VM is less than that of the host. Similarly, the detection time in high workloads is longer than in low workloads because higher workload leads to more processes contend for CPUs. In the worst case, the time of an attack to be successfully detected is about 37% of the time the attack required to complete. Above all, CBA-Detector can detect attacks in real time.

5.2   Accuracy in Detector

To answer Q-2, we test the accuracy of three classifiers generated in the offline phase and the real-time detector in the online phase, respectively. To evaluate the accuracy of classifiers, we measure TPR (True Positive Rate), FPR (False Positive Rate), recall, precision, F-Measure and ROC area of dec, xgb and mlp on offline feature vectors. As shown in Table 1, all the three models have over 98% precision and a few false positives.

Table 1. Performance evaluation of three classifiers on offline feature vectors

	TPR	FPR	Recall	Precision	F-Measure	ROC area
xgb	1.000000	0.000240	1.000000	0.992857	0.996416	0.999880
mlp	0.997302	0.000488	0.997302	0.985515	0.991374	0.998407
dec	1.000000	0.000288	1.000000	0.991441	0.995702	0.999856

Table 2. False positives during the online phase

	xgb	mlp	dec	Two models	Three models	sched_yield
w/o Pintools	2	7	10	6	1	0
w Pintools	0	0	0	0	0	0

To evaluate the real-time detector, we run 213 programs to test the false positives of CBA-Detector with or without Pintools. The 213 programs include benchmarks, Linux common commands and some applications like gedit. Benchmarks are used for evaluating the effectiveness of Pintools we developed because they use `rdtsc` or `rdtscp` instruction as well. Besides, concurrent applications of PARSEC, which invoke the system call `sched yield` multiple times, are used for testing the effectiveness of the strategy that relies on the system call `sched yield`. In Table 2, *two/three models* refers to two/three classifiers simultaneously misreport. Table 2 illustrates that CBA-Detector with Pintools can effectively eliminate false positives.

5.3 Performance

To answer *Q-3*, we first use the SPEC CPU2006 benchmark and PARSEC benchmark to measure the impact of CBA-Detector on different applications in the host machine. Then we measure the impact of CBA-Detector on web servers and a database in the virtual machine. We pin CBA-Detector to a single core and use the test input sets for SPEC and the simsmall input sets for PARSEC. Figures 6 and 7 show the results. The geometric mean of the overhead on applications of SPECCPU 2006 is 1.3% without the Pintools and 3.4% with the Pintools, while the geometric mean of the overhead on PARSEC is 4.4%.

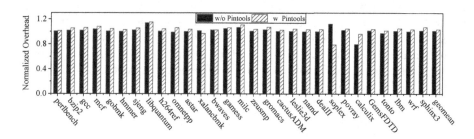

Fig. 6. The overhead of all applications in SPECCPU 2006

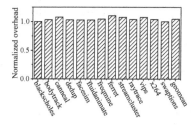

Fig. 7. Performance on PARSEC

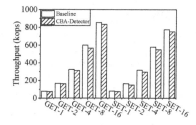

Fig. 8. Performance on Redis

To test the effects of CBA-Detector on web servers, we test Nginx and Apache via apache benchmark (ab) with a 1 MB static web page and different threads. Figure 5 shows the throughput of web servers. On the average, the overhead on Nginx and Apache is about 10.6% and 8.2%, respectively. The standard redis-benchmark is used for testing the throughput of SET and GET operations of Redis. We configure different numbers of threads for redis-benchmark and Fig. 8 depicts the results. On the average, CBA-Detector has about 4.8% overhead.

5.4   Discussion

In this section, we discuss the limitations, possible countermeasures and future work of CBA-Detector. First, our results prove that CBA-Detector can accurately detect attacks in real time. However, it does not exclude the rare cases where some benign programs may have similar instructions to attacks. In this case, CBA-Detector may misjudge these benign programs as attacks. To solve this problem, we suggest to adding these benign programs to the whitelist in advance. Second, a premeditated attack may evade CBA-Detector. For example, it may launch an attack after it is moved to Q_2 with loose surveillance. One possible solution is to randomly move some pids from Q_2 to Q_1 at a regular interval to further reduce the risk of missing attacks. Third, the Pintools we developed focus on the number of specific instructions because they are frequently used in attacks. We hope to find more interesting features of special instructions to detect attacks in the future. Forth, since the Pintools can accurately identify misjudgment of classifiers, we hope to automatically improve classifiers according to the feedback of Pintools so that CBA-Detector can detect attacks with better flexibility and adaptability in the future.

6   Related Work

Many studies attempted to detect cache-based side-channel attacks relying on HPCs. CloudRadar [18] analyzed hardware events obtained from HPCs to capture attacks in the virtual machines that are executing a cryptographic application. Chiappetta et al. [2] presented three real-time detection methods (correlation-based approach, anomaly detection and neural network) against Flush+Reload according to events collected with HPCs. NIGHTs-WATCH [11] employed machine learning techniques to analyze real-time data from HPCs to identify Flush+Reload and Flush+Flush under various realistic system load conditions. HexPADS [12] proposed a detection method against attacks by analyzing data collected from HPCs and performance metrics. CacheShield [1] adopted self-monitoring with the help of HPCs to detect attacks.

Detection methods rely on HPCs can detect attacks in real time, but inevitably have false positives. Other detection methods like SCADET [14], which introduced a methodology for detecting Prime+Probe by tracking to get memory-access behavior. It does not rely on HPCs but cannot detect attacks in real time. ZITF [16] uses Intel-PIN to tamper the time information of malicious processes, but it uses `perf` to filter benign processes with specific thresholds, which is not flexible and universal. Different from the above works, CBA-Detector uses machine learning techniques and combines HPCs with customized Pintools to detect Prime+Probe, Flush+Reload and Flush+Flush in real time, and it can effectively eliminate false positives at the instruction level.

7 Conclusion

This paper proposes an accurate detector called CBA-Detector to detect cache-based attacks in real time. CBA-Detector first employs machine learning techniques to model the features of hardware events collected with HPCs. Then it combines the models with Pintools to identify attacks in real time and eliminate false positives at the instruction level. Our experiments show that CBA-Detector can accurately detect cache-based attacks before they complete while introducing 4.4% overhead on PARSEC and about 10% overhead on web server.

Acknowlegements. This work was supported by National Natural Science Foundation of China (No. 61772204, No. 61732014).

References

1. Briongos, S., Irazoqui, G., Malagón, P., Eisenbarth, T.: CacheShield: detecting cache attacks through self-observation. In: CODASPY 2018, pp. 224–235 (2018)
2. Chiappetta, M., Savas, E., Yilmaz, C.: Real time detection of cache-based side-channel attacks using hardware performance counters. Appl. Soft Comput. **49**, 1162–1174 (2016)
3. Das, S., Werner, J., Antonakakis, M., Polychronakis, M., Monrose, F.: SoK: the challenges, pitfalls, and perils of using hardware performance counters for security. In: 2019 IEEE Symposium on Security and Privacy (SP) (2019)
4. Gruss, D., Lettner, J., Schuster, F., Ohrimenko, O., Haller, I., Costa, M.: Strong and efficient cache side-channel protection using hardware transactional memory. In: USENIX Security, pp. 217–233 (2017)
5. Gruss, D., Maurice, C., Wagner, K., Mangard, S.: Flush+Flush: a fast and stealthy cache attack. In: Caballero, J., Zurutuza, U., Rodríguez, R.J. (eds.) DIMVA 2016. LNCS, vol. 9721, pp. 279–299. Springer, Cham (2016). https://doi.org/10.1007/978-3-319-40667-1_14
6. Kim, T., Peinado, M., Mainar-Ruiz, G.: STEALTHMEM: system-level protection against cache-based side channel attacks in the cloud. In: USENIX Security, pp. 189–204 (2012)
7. Kocher, P., et al.: Spectre attacks: exploiting speculative execution. CoRR abs/1801.01203 (2018)
8. Lipp, M., et al.: Meltdown. CoRR abs/1801.01207 (2018)
9. Liu, F., et al.: CATalyst: defeating last-level cache side channel attacks in cloud computing. In: HPCA, pp. 406–418 (2016)
10. Liu, F., Yarom, Y., Ge, Q., Heiser, G., Lee, R.B.: Last-level cache side-channel attacks are practical. In: SP, pp. 605–622 (2015)

11. Mushtaq, M., Akram, A., Bhatti, M.K., Chaudhry, M., Lapotre, V., Gogniat, G.: NIGHTs-WATCH: a cache-based side-channel intrusion detector using hardware performance counters. In: HASP, pp. 1:1–1:8 (2018)
12. Payer, M.: HexPADS: a platform to detect "Stealth" attacks. In: Caballero, J., Bodden, E., Athanasopoulos, E. (eds.) ESSoS 2016. LNCS, vol. 9639, pp. 138–154. Springer, Cham (2016). https://doi.org/10.1007/978-3-319-30806-7_9
13. Intel Pin: Intel pin dynamic binary instrumentation tool (2012). https://software. intel.com/en-us/articles/pin-a-dynamic-binary-instrumentation-tool. Accessed 20 Apr 2019
14. Sabbagh, M., Fei, Y., Wahl, T., Ding, A.A.: SCADET: a side-channel attack detection tool for tracking Prime+Probe. In: ICCAD 2018, p. 107 (2018)
15. Terpstra, D., Jagode, H., You, H., Dongarra, J.J.: Collecting performance data with PAPI-C. In: Müller, M., Resch, M., Schulz, A., Nagel, W. (eds.) International Workshop on Parallel Tools for High Performance Computing 2009, pp. 157–173. Springer, Heidelberg (2010). https://doi.org/10.1007/978-3-642-11261-4_11
16. Wang, Z.H., Peng, S.H., Guo, X.Y., Jiang, W.B.: Zero in and TimeFuzz: detection and mitigation of cache side-channel attacks. In: Lanet, J.-L., Toma, C. (eds.) SECITC 2018. LNCS, vol. 11359, pp. 410–424. Springer, Cham (2019). https:// doi.org/10.1007/978-3-030-12942-2_31
17. Yarom, Y., Falkner, K.: FLUSH+RELOAD: a high resolution, low noise, L3 cache side-channel attack. In: USENIX Security, pp. 719–732 (2014)
18. Zhang, T., Zhang, Y., Lee, R.B.: CloudRadar: a real-time side-channel attack detection system in clouds. In: Monrose, F., Dacier, M., Blanc, G., Garcia-Alfaro, J. (eds.) RAID 2016. LNCS, vol. 9854, pp. 118–140. Springer, Cham (2016). https:// doi.org/10.1007/978-3-319-45719-2_6

An Efficient Log Parsing Algorithm Based on Heuristic Rules

Lin Zhang[1], Xueshuo Xie[2], Kunpeng Xie[2], Zhi Wang[1], Ye Lu[2(✉)], and Yujun Zhang[3]

[1] College of Cyber Science, Nankai University, Tianjin, China
zl@mail.nankai.edu.cn, zwang@nankai.edu.cn
[2] College of Computer Science, Nankai University, Tianjin, China
{xueshuoxie,1511220}@mail.nankai.edu.cn, luye@nankai.edu.cn
[3] Institute of Computing Technology, Chinese Academy of Sciences, Beijing, China
zhmj@ict.ac.cn

Abstract. Log files usually contain very rich running information of the software system, which can be used for anomaly detection, performance modeling, and failure diagnosis, etc. In a large-scale deployment system, log records are always unstructured and can not directly use for log analysis. Log parsing, as a key prerequisite for log analysis, converts unstructured log records into structured event templates by extracting the constant portion of the raw log. Traditionally, log parsing can be achieved by manually using the regular expression, which requires many experts knowledge and has very low efficiency. Therefore, the accuracy and efficiency of log parsing are very important, especially in large-scale distributed systems. In this paper, we propose an efficient algorithm namely CLF (Clustering based on Length and First token) for extracting log event templates from raw log based on heuristic rules. The CLF algorithm works through a 3-step process: clustering unstructured logs based on heuristic rules, clustering again according to specific separation rules and finally generating event templates. Finally, we used 7 data sets to evaluate the performance of CLF and compared with three state-of-the-art log parser algorithms, where CLF ranks higher on most of the data sets and also has advantages in execution time.

Keywords: Log parsing · Log analysis · Clustering · Algorithms

1 Introduction

Web services, instant messaging, search engines, etc. are very common in modern computer networks, and they are an indispensable part of our lives, so the reliability of these systems is very important. In order to ensure the reliability of the systems, it is necessary to analyze the logs produced by the system at runtime that they can be used for abnormal detection [1–4], fault diagnosis [5–7], and performance monitoring [8,9].

© Springer Nature Switzerland AG 2019
P.-C. Yew et al. (Eds.): APPT 2019, LNCS 11719, pp. 123–134, 2019.
https://doi.org/10.1007/978-3-030-29611-7_10

When performing some analysis on a log file, first the event corresponding to each log entry needs to be known. Log entries typically include a timestamp and an actual log message, where the timestamp records the time at which the event occurred, and the log message records the operational information associated with the event. For example, there is a log entry: '081109 203519 145 INFO dfs.DataNode$PacketResponder:PacketResponder 1 for block blk_-16089 terminating'. In this log entry, 'PacketResponder 1 for block blk_16089 terminating' is the log message part. Log messages usually consist of two parts, a fixed part and a variable part. Log messages belonging to the same event type have the same fixed part (eg 'PacketResponder', 'for', 'block', 'terminating' constitute a fixed part), and Variable parts (eg '1', 'blk_3886' are variables) may change as events occur. The template for this log message should be 'PacketResponder '$< * >$' for block '$< * >$' terminating'.

Because developers write free-text log print statements in the source code, log messages are unstructured when different event logs are output. However, most log analysis tools and data mining models require structured log input and then make more accurate judgments about the system's operational information. Therefore, when performing log analysis, the first step is to resolve the unstructured log into a structured log [10,11]. Extracting the log message templates from the log file not only facilitates subsequent log analysis, but also has prominent advantages in the following aspects: (1) It is possible to use a more concise and compact log message template to represent log entries and save memory; (2) log entries are easier to query and summarize.

In general, automatic identification of log messages still requires manual operation. It matches the regular expression to extract the template, and the regular expression is created and updated according to the log print statement in the program source code. When there are a lot of log print statements in the source code of the program, manually creating regular expressions can be time-consuming and labor-intensive. Of course, there are other ways to statically analyze the application source code, look up the log record statement, and extract the template from the print operation. But the definition of static analysis will be cumbersome and requires extensive knowledge of recording techniques, which is not easy in different programming languages and frameworks. Both of the above methods require access to the source code of the program, but this permission is not common, which will become a limitation of some log analysis. In the case where the program source code is not accessible, there is still a way to extract the template of the log message. For example, LKE [9], LenMa [12] and MoLFI [13], etc., they use the black-box strategy that relies on clustering techniques or evolutionary algorithm to automatically extract templates for log messages from log files. The log message template extracted by the algorithm should balance the under-fitting and over-fitting problems. That is, in a log file, (1) whether each log message template is too general, and logs of different events correspond to the same log message template; (2) whether each log message is too special, and the log indicating the same event corresponds to multiple log message templates. On this basis, the accuracy rate and time efficiency of the log parsing algorithm are measured. Our experiments show that the accuracy and efficiency of these algorithms are low.

In this paper, we propose the CLF algorithm, which uses heuristic-based clustering techniques to efficiently parse log files. The rest of this paper is organized as follows: Sect. 2 discusses the work related to log parsing and the published algorithms. Section 3 outlines the proposed algorithm. Section 4 reports a description of the CLF assessment and experimental results. Finally, Sect. 5 presents the conclusion.

2   Related Work

Log parsing is a process that transforms unstructured log messages into structured log messages. In particular, the log parser matches each log message with a log event. In this section, we discuss previous related work in the area of event log clustering and message type extraction [14–16]. We also discuss the CLF algorithm in multiple perspectives.

From the SLCT [17] algorithm released in 2003 to the newly released MoLFI [13] algorithm, a total of 13 recently published log parsing methods to implement the function of automatically identifying log messages. The existing log parsing algorithms are mainly implemented in the following ways: clustering, frequency pattern mining, and heuristic. The algorithms that rely on clustering for log parsing are: LKE [9], LogSig [18], SHISO [19], LenMa [12] and LogMine [20]. These algorithms use machine learning techniques. They cluster log entries by calculating the similarity between log entries (such as weighted edit distance) and then extract templates. Algorithms for mining using frequency patterns are: SLCT, LFA [21] and LogCluster [22]. These three algorithms traverse the log data, then group logs into several clusters based on the frequency of occurrences of words in each log entry (or words at a fixed location), and finally extract the message template. The following algorithms are based on heuristic rules: AEL [23], IPLoM [24] and Drain [25]. The developers of these three algorithms use heuristic rules to parse the logs by observing the characteristics of the log messages. The latest algorithm MoLFI [13] applies the Non-dominated Sorting Genetic Algorithm II (NSGA-II [26]) on a given log file to search the space of solutions for a Pareto optimal set of message templates. It formalizes the log parsing as a multiple-objective optimization problem and utilizes a genetic algorithm to solve it. Different log parsers can use different log parsing strategies. Of course, these log parsers can get results without accessing the source code. The CLF method we propose uses a clustering technique that relies on heuristic rules. Data clustering [17,18,27,28] is a data mining technique, which classifies data into clusters. The members of each cluster are related, and the members of different clusters have large differences. Clustering is very useful in the interpretation and classification of datasets, and it can be used as the first step in log parsing.

To adapt the various scenarios of log parsing, developers have designed two main modes of log parsing, i.e., offline and online. The offline log parser processes the log files in batch mode, and it needs the software system to provide all the logs before log parsing. Instead, the online log parser processes the log messages one by one in a stream. Among the log parsers that are offline and online, Drain is better in the online log parsers, and IPLoM is better in the offline log parsers. Drain is based on a fixed-depth tree structure. When a new raw log message arrives, it first searches for an appropriate log group from the nodes in the tree. If an appropriate log group is found, the log will be added. Otherwise, a new log group will be created. IPLoM employs an iterative partition strategy, which partitions log messages by event size, token position and mapping relation.

Most of the log parsers mentioned above are complicated to process log files that they generally need to traverse the log files multiple times or traverse their own data processing models multiple times or perform a large number of calculations. Although complex processing can usually improve the accuracy rate, it loses its advantage in terms of time efficiency. The CLF is not complicated to process the log file and it has great advantages in time efficiency under the premise of ensuring the correct rate. It uses clustering technology, which is an offline parser. It clusters the logs based on whether the first word of each log message is the same and the length of each log message. Because in general, the first word of the event message represents an important feature of the event, and the length of the log message (the number of tokens) of the same event is the same. On this basis, coarse-grained clustering is performed, followed by fine-grained clustering by special separation rules and then the CLF algorithm can accurately group similar logs. Such an operation does not require traversing the log file multiple times or traversing its own model multiple times, so the CLF algorithm can parse the log file at an extremely fast rate. Our experiments show that CLF is indeed the fastest log parser and has a high accuracy rate on different data sets.

3   The CLF Algorithm

In this section, we give a detailed description of our proposed algorithm. The CLF (clustering based on length and first token) algorithm is designed as a log data parsing algorithm, it uses clustering technology and heuristic rules. An outline of the three steps of CLF is given in Fig. 1. For example, when a log file needs to be parsed, as shown in Table 1, CLF will preprocess it with simple regular expressions based on domain knowledge. Then we group logs into clusters based on whether the first word of each log message is the same and the length of each log message. Then CLF separates the classified groups again using specific separation rules. Finally, CLF extracts the log messages templates.

The preprocessing is simple that the specific parameters are erased by empirical rules. For example, in network-related logs, the frequently occurring IP addresses are the parameters to be erased. In general, this simple preprocessing will improve the accuracy of the log parsing algorithm. The CLF preprocesses log files by defining some regular expressions to match these parameters and erasing them.

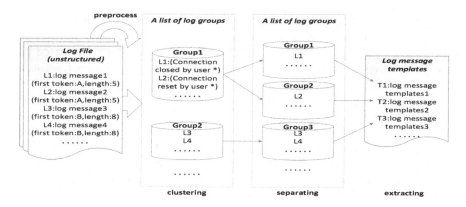

Fig. 1. The log file will first be preprocessed by erasing some parameters. The first step of the algorithm is to cluster the log messages based on whether the first token and length are the same. The second step is to identify constants and variables and then do the in-group separation. The last step is to extract the common parts of the log messages within the group as the log message templates.

Table 1. Raw log messages

	Log messages
1	Connection closed by user 72480
2	Connection reset by user 72480
3	Invalid user test9 from 173.234.31.186
4	Invalid user adm from 173.234.31.186
5	Invalid user John from 173.234.31.186
6	Invalid user Mike from 173.234.31.186
7	PacketResponder 2 for block blk_-6670 terminating

After the CLF preprocesses the log file, it performs the three-step processing to complete the parsing, as follows:

3.1 Step 1: Clustering

The CLF algorithm first clusters log messages based on whether their first word is the same or not and then clusters log messages according to their length.

For each line of log messages, we take the first word as a flag. We don't consider words in other positions. The log messages with the same first word can be clustered into a group. In general, the first word of a log message represents important information (because a process name is printed here normally), such as the first word of a warning message would be "Warning" and the first word of an error message would be "Error". Even if the first words are the same, they may not be the same type of log event. In this case, we need to cluster the groups again according to the lengths of the log messages because different print statements usually have different numbers of words. When the first word is the same, and the different lengths of the logs are used for grouping, the related log messages can be more accurately divided into one group, thereby extracting a representative template.

The log messages in each group are basically similar, but there may still be cases that the log messages output by different log print statements have the same first word and length. For example, in a log file, all log entries record only two events, one for successful connection and the other for failed connection. This means that these logs are output by two print statements. Then the difference between the two print statements is probably that one word is different at a certain position, such as one is 'success' and the other is 'fail'. If the word ('success' or 'fail') is not the first word, then the previous clustering step will classify the logs into the same category. This problem will be solved by the next separation step.

After clustering, the examples mentioned earlier as shown in Table 2.

Table 2. CLF step 1: clustering by the first token of log messages and the length of the messages

Group	Log messages
1	Connection closed by user $< * >$
	Connection reset by user $< * >$
2	Invalid user test9 from $< * >$
	Invalid user adm from $< * >$
	Invalid user John from $< * >$
	Invalid user Mike from $< * >$
3	PacketResponder $< * >$ for block $< * >$ terminating

3.2   Step 2: Separating

Each log message contains constants and variable components. The constants contain the fixed information of the print statement and are also the keywords of the log. The variables change with the occurrence of the event when the system is running. After accurately clustering all the log messages, the common part of each log message in the group is the log message template that we want to finally get. But after step 1, the grouping of log messages is not accurate. Because some constants are mistaken for variables. How to accurately separate constants and variables is what step 2 does.

We make statistics on words in all positions of the log messages and set a separation threshold. Assuming that there are n different tokens at a certain position of each log message. When n is greater than the separation threshold, the token at that position is considered a variable, otherwise, it is a constant. We do not need to make any changes to the log messages when the token at a certain location is considered a variable, because the token will change directly to the $< * >$ wildcard due to differences when extracting the common part as a template. When a token at a position is considered a constant, we should regroup the log messages in this group according to the tokens at this position, and group the log messages with the same token into one group. This continues the grouping operation more than once, the algorithm will first save the public token sequence within the group, and then traverse the above operations for other tokens.

When step 2 is completed, the logs in each group are already very similar. For a group, the CLF algorithm will assume that the log messages within the group are printed by the same log print statement. The next step is to extract the public part of each group as a template, which is the third step.

After Separating, the examples mentioned earlier as shown in Table 3.

Table 3. CLF step 2: separating by the number of different tokens in the same position of the log messages

Group	Log messages
1	Connection closed by user $< * >$
2	Connection reset by user $< * >$
3	Invalid user test9 from $< * >$
	Invalid user adm from $< * >$
	Invalid user John from $< * >$
	Invalid user Mike from $< * >$
4	PacketResponder $< * >$ for block $< * >$ terminating

3.3   Step 3: Extracting Template

After the first and second steps, all the log messages have been clustered into different groups, and extracting the template for each group is the third step. For a group, its template should be the same part between each log messages and other log messages in the group, that is, the template consisting of constants. The different tokens between each log messages are variable components, which should be deleted and represented by wildcards $< * >$.

After Extracting, the examples mentioned earlier as shown in Table 4.

Table 4. CLF step 3: extracting by the common part of each log message in the group

Group	Log Templates
1	Connection closed by user $< * >$
2	Connection reset by user $< * >$
3	Invalid user $< * >$ from $< * >$
4	PacketResponder $< * >$ for block $< * >$ terminating

4   Evaluation

We have implemented the proposed algorithm in Python 2.7. The CLF algorithm can find all the message types that may exist in a given log file. In this section, we report the accuracy and time efficiency assessment of the CLF algorithm in identifying log message formats. We first describe the experimental settings. Then, We want to assess the performance of CLF in comparison with state-of-the-art techniques (Drain and IPLoM) and the newly released log parser (MoLFI), in terms of accuracy and efficiency.

4.1   Experimental Settings

Dataset. To evaluate the CLF, we used seven different benchmark datasets: seven datasets are publicly available and come from the real world, and have been used in previous work for log message format identification issues. These datasets were released by [29], they are HDFS (Hadoop Distributed File System), Thunderbird (Thunderbird Supercomputer), Hadoop (Hadoop MapReduce), openSSH (OpenSSH server log), Apache (Apache HTTP Server), HPC (High Performance Cluster), Spark (Large-Scale Data Processing Platform), and each data set contains 2000 log entries. We used the ground truth defined by [29] and publicly available from their replication package.

All log parsers have been run multiple times, we used the average result as the evaluation criteria and collected the generated log message templates. For the results obtained by the algorithm, we use F-measure [30] to evaluate the accuracy of log parsing methods. The evaluation indicators often have the following points: Accuracy, Precision, Recall and F1-Measure. To measure the accuracy, we used the metrics used in previous studies [25,30], i.e., $Accuracy = \frac{TP+TN}{TP+TN+FP+FN}$, $Precision = \frac{TP}{TP+FP}$, $Recall = \frac{TP}{TP+FN}$, and $F1\_Measure = \frac{2*Precision*Recall}{Precision+Recall}$. That a true positive (TP) decision assigns two log messages with the same log event to the same log group;a true negative (TN) decision assigns two log messages with the different log event to different log groups; a false positive (FP) decision assigns two log messages with different log events to the same log group; and a false negative (FN) decision assigns two log messages with the same log event to different log groups.

We use Accuracy and F1_Measure to evaluate the accuracy of each algorithm. These two standards are typical evaluation criteria. In addition to these 7 data sets, we also selected HDFS data sets of different sizes, which are 1 kb, 10 kb, 100 kb, 1 mb, 10 mb and 100 mb. They are used to test the execution time of each algorithm and compare whether the CLF algorithm is better than other algorithms in terms of time efficiency. We ran all the experiments on a Windows server with an Intel(R) Core(TM) I7-6700 CPU and 8 GB RAM, running Window7 with 64 bits.

4.2 Accuracy and F1_Measure

Accuracy is a major issue in existing log parsing studies that demonstrate how well the log parser matches raw log messages with the correct log events. In addition, inaccurate log parsers can greatly hinder the effectiveness of downstream log mining tasks.

In this section, we evaluate the accuracy of the MoLFI, Drain, IPLoM and CLF algorithms on seven data sets. The evaluation results are shown in Table 5. The columns "Acc", "FM", and "T" indicate accuracy, F_measure, and execution time (in seconds), respectively. In our results, because the Apache server's logging format is simple and easy to understand, these log parsers can resolve Apache datasets 100% accurately. Similarly, they all have high accuracy and F-measure on HDFS datasets because HDFS datasets do not have complex structures and formats. We observed that for most data sets, CLF achieved the best accuracy and F-measure. Drain and IPLoM have also achieved high accuracy because of their specially designed heuristic rules. The MoLFI algorithm is the slowest in terms of efficiency because it uses an iterative algorithm. Because of the special clustering rules and separation rule, CLF is very effective in processing log files and achieves the best overall accuracy. On average, Drain is less accurate than CLF, followed by IPLoM and finally MoLFI. In terms of F-measure, these four log parsers all scored well, which indicates that they have a high recall rate and precision rate.

Table 5. Accuracy (Acc), F1_Measure (FM) and execution time (T(s)) of the approaches

Dataset	MoLFI			Drain			IPLoM			CLF		
	Acc	FM	T(s)	Acc	FM	T(s)	Acc	FM	T(s)	Acc	FM	T(s)
HDFS	0.99	0.99	3.18	0.99	0.99	0.26	1	1	0.24	**1**	1	0.16
Thunderbird	0.65	0.99	40.9	**0.95**	0.99	0.25	0.66	0.99	0.25	0.93	0.99	0.26
Hadoop	0.94	0.99	28.57	0.94	0.99	0.25	0.95	0.99	0.28	**0.96**	0.99	0.21
OpenSSH	0.48	0.99	6.42	0.78	0.99	0.25	**0.80**	0.99	0.23	**0.80**	0.99	0.22
Apache	1	1	1.44	1	1	0.22	1	1	0.21	1	1	0.17
HPC	0.67	0.97	16.67	0.88	0.99	0.24	0.82	0.97	0.20	**0.91**	0.99	0.12
Spark	0.41	0.51	203.8	0.92	0.99	0.25	0.92	0.99	0.23	**0.98**	0.99	0.27

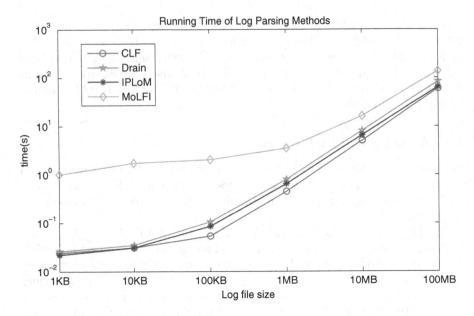

Fig. 2. Running time of log parsing methods

4.3 Efficiency

The efficiency of a log parser is an important aspect to consider when dealing with large-scale log data. We use a private HDFS data set and slice it into 1 kb, 10 kb, 100 kb, 1 mb, 10 mb, and 100 mb. These different sized data sets are used to test the efficiency of the log parser, and we record the time it takes for each log parser to complete the entire parsing process. The logarithmic scale used, as shown in Fig. 2. CLF requires less runtime than other log parsers. The newly released log parser MoLFI uses an iterative evolutionary algorithm, so it is always slower than Drain, IPLoM and CLF, regardless of the size of the data set. MoLFI uses novel ideas to implement algorithms, but it is not good in terms of time efficiency. Drain and IPLoM are the most efficient log parsers in the currently published log parser. CLF and their running time are almost the same when the size of the data set is less than 1MB. But as the size of the data set increases, the runtime of the CLF grows much slower than Drain and IPLoM. Specifically, the CLF only needs to resolve 10 MB of HDFS log messages in 5 s and 100 MB of HDFS log messages in 59 s. It greatly improves the runtime of log parsers. CLF runs faster than other log parsers for a number of reasons. First, the clustering step of CLF has fewer traversal for log files, this reduces memory usage and reduces processing time for log files. Second, CLF enjoys linear time complexity. Because CLF and IPLoM are offline log parsers, there is less processing time for log files than online log parser Drain. As the size of the data set continues to expand, the advantages of CLF in processing time will become more apparent.

5 Conclusion

Log parsing is critical for log analysis based on software systems. This paper proposes a log parsing algorithm, CLF, which relies on simple rules to infer log message templates. An experimental result involving multiple real-world datasets shows that the CLF algorithm has higher precision than common log parsing tools.

Acknowledgment. This work is partially supported by the National Key Research and Development Program of China (2016YFC0400709), the Next Generation Internet Technology Innovation Project of CERNET (NGII20180306), the Science and Technology Commission of Tianjin Binhai New Area (BHXQKJXM-PT-ZJSHJ-2017005), the Natural Science Foundation of Tianjin (18YFYZCG00060) and Nankai University (91922299).

References

1. Bertero, C., Roy, M., Sauvanaud, C., Tredan, G.: Experience report: log mining using natural language processing and application to anomaly detection. In: IEEE International Symposium on Software Reliability Engineering (2017)
2. Goldstein, M., Raz, D., Segall, I.: Log-based behavioral differencing. In: IEEE International Symposium on Software Reliability Engineering, Experience report (2017)
3. Kc, K., Gu, X.: ELT: Efficient log-based troubleshooting system for cloud computing infrastructures. In: Reliable Distributed Systems (2011)
4. Ren, R., Fu, X., Zhan, J., Zhou, W.: LogMaster: Mining event correlations in logs of large scale cluster systems. In: IEEE Symposium on Reliable Distributed Systems (2012)
5. Zou, D.Q.: Uilog: improving log-based fault diagnosis by log analysis. J. Comput. Sci. Technol. **31**(5), 1038–1052 (2016)
6. Wong, W.E., Debroy, V., Golden, R., Xu, X., Thuraisingham, B.: Effective software fault localization using an RBF neural network. IEEE Transact. Reliab. **61**(1), 149–169 (2012)
7. Reidemeister, T., Jiang, M., Ward, P.A.S.: Mining unstructured log files for recurrent fault diagnosis. In: IFIP/IEEE International Symposium on Integrated Network Management (2011)
8. Nagaraj, K., Neville, J., Killian, C.: Structured comparative analysis of systems logs to diagnose performance problems. In: USENIX Conference on Networked Systems Design and Implementation (2012)
9. Fu, Q., Lou, J.G., Wang, Y., Li, J.: Execution anomaly detection in distributed systems through unstructured log analysis. In: IEEE International Conference on Data Mining (2009)
10. Lou, J.G., Fu, Q., Yang, S., Xu, Y., Li, J.: Mining invariants from console logs for system problem detection. In: Proceedings of USENIX ATC, pp. 231–244 (2010)
11. Wei, X., Ling, H., Fox, A., Patterson, D.A., Jordan, M.I.: Detecting large-scale system problems by mining console logs. In: ACM SIGOPS Symposium on Operating Systems Principles (2009)
12. Shima, K.: Length matters: clustering system log messages using length of words (2016)

13. Messaoudi, S., Panichella, A., Bianculli, D., Briand, L., Sasnauskas, R.: A search-based approach for accurate identification of log message formats. pp. 167–177 (2018)
14. Ma, H., Hellerstein, J.L.: Mining partially periodic event patterns with unknown periods. In: International Conference on Data Engineering (2000)
15. Zheng, Q., Xu, K., Lv, W., Ma, S.: Intelligent search of correlated alarms from database containing noise data. In: Network Operations and Management Symposium (2001)
16. Stearley, J.: Towards informatic analysis of syslogs. In: IEEE International Conference on Cluster Computing (2004)
17. Vaarandi, R.: A data clustering algorithm for mining patterns from event logs. In: IP Operations and Management (2003)
18. Liang, T., Tao, L., Perng, C.S.: LogSig: generating system events from raw textual logs. In: ACM International Conference on Information and Knowledge Management (2011)
19. Mizutani, M.: Incremental mining of system log format. In: IEEE International Conference on Services Computing (2013)
20. Hamooni, H., Debnath, B., Xu, J., Hui, Z., Mueen, A.: Logmine: Fast pattern recognition for log analytics. In: ACM International on Conference on Information and Knowledge Management (2016)
21. Nagappan, M., Vouk, M.A.: Abstracting log lines to log event types for mining software system logs. In: Mining Software Repositories (2010)
22. Vaarandi, R., Pihelgas, M.: LogCluster - a data clustering and pattern mining algorithm for event logs. In: International Conference on Network and Service Management (2016)
23. Jiang, Z.M., Hassan, A.E., Flora, P., Hamann, G.: Abstracting execution logs to execution events for enterprise applications (short paper). pp. 181–186, August 2008
24. Makanju, A., Zincir-Heywood, A.N., Milios, E.E.: A lightweight algorithm for message type extraction in system application logs. IEEE Transact. Knowl. Data Eng. **24**(11), 1921–1936 (2012)
25. He, P., Zhu, J., Zheng, Z., Lyu, M.R.: Drain: an online log parsing approach with fixed depth tree. In: IEEE International Conference on Web Services (2017)
26. Deb, K., Pratap, A., Agarwal, S., Meyarivan, T.: A fast and elitist multiobjective genetic algorithm: NSGA-II. IEEE Transact. Evol. Comput. **6**(2), 182–197 (2002)
27. Makanju, A., Zincir-Heywood, A.N., Milios, E.E.: Clustering event logs using iterative partitioning. In: ACM SIGKDD International Conference on Knowledge Discovery and Data Mining (2009)
28. Liang, T., Tao, L.: LogTree: a framework for generating system events from raw textual logs. In: IEEE International Conference on Data Mining (2011)
29. Zhu, J., He, S., Liu, J., He, P., Lyu, M.R.: Tools and benchmarks for automated log parsing (2018)
30. Manning, C.D., Raghavan, P., Schütze, H.: Introduction to Information Retrieval (2010)

Distribution Forest: An Anomaly Detection Method Based on Isolation Forest

Chengfei Yao[1], Xiaoqing Ma[1], Biao Chen[1], Xiaosong Zhao[2],
and Gang Bai[1(✉)]

[1] College of Computer Science, Nankai University, Tianjin, China
2120160400@mail.nankai.edu.cn, baigang@nankai.edu.cn
[2] Tianjin Public Security Profession College, Tianjin, China

Abstract. Anomaly detection refers to finding patterns in the data that do not meet expectations. Anomaly detection has a variety of application domains and scenarios, such as network intrusion detection, fraud detection and fault detection. This paper proposes a new anomaly detection method Distribution Forest (dForest) inspired by Isolation Forest (iForest). dForest builds an ensemble of special binary trees called distribution tree (dTree). The basic idea of our method is to guide the building of dTree by the distribution of data at each node. And each node of dTree is treated as a subspace of input space. When dForest is built, the anomalies have a shorter path length than the normal instances.

dForest has a different explanation from other methods. Compared with iForest, LOF and iNNE, the proposed method achieves competitive results in terms of AUC on different benchmark datasets. Also, dForest performs well in both semi-supervised and unsupervised anomaly detection modes.

Keywords: Anomaly detection · Mahalanobis distance · Isolation forest

1 Introduction

Anomaly detection is an important branch of data mining tasks and has received extensive attention. Anomaly detection refers to the problem of finding patterns in data that do not meet expectations [1]. These unexpected patterns refers to outliers, noisy, observations, events, items and so on. Anomaly detection plays an important role in many application domains and scenarios, such as network intrusion detection, fraud detection and fault detection.

The history of research on anomaly detection dates back to the 19th century, and there exists a variety of techniques in this field. There are several types of anomaly detection methods included clustering-based methods [2], density-based methods [3], distance-based methods [4] and other method [7, 8]. The majority of these methods have high time complexity and memory costs. Among them, isolation forest (iForest) is an isolation-based anomaly detection method proposed by Liu and Ting in [5, 6]. iForest isolates anomalies through axis-parallel divisions rather than profiles normal instances. The main advantage of iForest is that it has a linear time complexity with low memory requirements. The limitation of iForest is that it is not sensitive to local

© Springer Nature Switzerland AG 2019
P.-C. Yew et al. (Eds.): APPT 2019, LNCS 11719, pp. 135–147, 2019.
https://doi.org/10.1007/978-3-030-29611-7_11

anomalies for the global scores [15]. This paper proposes a new method to solve the above problems in the framework of iForest.

Similar to iForest, dForest builds an ensemble of dTrees. In the process of building a dTree, several attributes are randomly selected at each node to form a subspace of the feature space. Then the division of each node is performed on the subspace. In the division of each node, we introduce covariance estimation and use Mahalanobis distance to determine a hyperellipsoid. The points inside the hyperellipsoid are divided into the left child, and the points outside the hyperellipsoid are divided into the right child. Each internal node is divided according to the distribution of local area, so that the possible normal instances and anomalous instances are divided into different branches as much as possible. Therefore, the anomalies is easier to be divided into leaf nodes than normal instances. Compared with other method, dForest have the following advantages:

(1) dForest makes full use of multi-dimensional information. At each node, several attributes are randomly selected. A large number of attribute combinations are used to form different subspaces. The data are mapped into those different low-dimensional subspaces.

(2) dForest works well in both semi-supervised and unsupervised mode. In the case of unsupervised anomaly detection, the normal instances and the anomalous instances are distinguished according to the Mahalanobis distance between the instance and the local distribution on different subspaces. In the case of semi-supervised anomaly detection, the boundary of the local distribution of each subspace is considered as the location where the anomaly may appear.

(3) dForest has an intuitive and clear explanation. At each node, the data are projected onto the subspace determined by randomly selected attributes. The nodes are divided according to the distribution of data on the subspace. In different sub-spaces, normal instances and anomalies are constantly distinguished according to the distribution.

The rest of this paper is organized as follows. Section 2 summarizes the related work briefly. Section 3 introduces the process and details of the proposed method. Section 4 mainly provides the results of comparison with other methods and other related experiments. Finally, Sect. 5 briefly gives conclusion.

2   Related Work

According to whether the labels is available, the anomaly detection techniques can be classified into the following three types.

Supervised Anomaly Detection. The kinds of techniques trains a model for normal vs. anomaly classes using the data that have been labeled. But the supervised anomaly detection techniques faced two major challenges. First, the normal instances and anomalous instances are unbalanced. Second, obtaining accurate labels is very difficult, especially for anomalous instances.

Semi-supervised Anomaly Detection. The related techniques assume that only normal instances have been label in training data. Generally, semi-supervised anomaly detection techniques train a model for normal data and treat data that does not conform to the model as anomalies.

Unsupervised Anomaly Detection. The techniques in this category do not require data to be labeled and are widely used. But it usually assumes that the number of normal instances is much larger than the number of anomalous instances.

The proposed method in this paper is mainly performed in the second and third cases: training with normal instances only or training with unlabeled data. According to the principle, the anomaly detection techniques can be divided into the following types.

Clustering-Based Anomaly Detection Techniques. The clustering-based anomaly detection techniques are based on the following recognitions: Normal instances belong to a certain cluster, and anomalies do not belong to any cluster. Or the normal instances belong to a relatively large cluster, while the anomalies belong to a relatively small cluster. The advantage of those techniques is that they can work in unsupervised mode. The limitation is that the performance mainly depend on the clustering algorithms.

Density-Based Anomaly Detection Techniques. The techniques in this category assume that an instance with low density is more likely to be an anomaly, and one with dense density is declared to be a normal instance. A well-known method density-based is local outlier factor (LOF). The key advantage of density-based anomaly detection techniques is that they are unsupervised techniques and doesn't need any assumptions about the distribution of the data. The disadvantage is that most of those techniques need to find neighbors and calculate distances, so the time complexity is relatively high.

Isolation-Based Anomaly Detection Techniques. The basic idea of isolation-based anomaly detection techniques is that anomalies are easier to be isolated than normal instances. The techniques isolates anomalies rather than profiles normal instances.

The first isolation-based method is iForest. iForest build an ensemble of isolation trees (iTree). An iTree is a special binary tree built from a subsample. Each internal node in the iTree is divided according to randomly selected thresholds on randomly selected attribute.

For a test instance x, the path length $h(x)$ in each iTree is collected at first and the average path length $E(h(x))$ is calculated. Since the number of the instances in leaf node may be greater than 1, the path length $h(x)$ needs to add the height of the subtree built using the data in leaf node. For the data of size n, the expected average path length $c(n)$ can be expressed as follows.

$$c(n) = 2H(n-1) - \frac{2(n-1)}{n} \tag{1}$$

$$H(i) = ln(i) + 0.5772156649 \tag{2}$$

Then the anomaly score s of x is calculated as the Eq. (3). The closer the score s is to 1, the more likely x is to be an anomaly. The closer the score s is to 0, the more likely x is to be a normal instance.

$$s(x, n) = 2^{-\frac{E(h(x))}{c(n)}} \tag{3}$$

iForest has a linear time complexity with low memory requirements, and can achieve high precision in many problems. Inspired by iForest, this paper proposes a new anomaly detection method, called Distribution Forest (dForest).

3   Our Method

From a different perspective, this paper proposes a new method for anomaly detection. Each node of the tree is treated as a subspace of the feature space. The data are divided in the subspace, the data at the center of the distribution are assigned to the left child, and the data at the edge of the distribution are divided into the right child. Each internal node of the binary tree contains part of the data, so it can be regarded as the distribution of local areas. Through the continuous splitting of the nodes, the normal instances and the anomalous instances are continuously distinguished in different subspaces. Less data are divided into right child so that the anomalies reach the leaf nodes faster. Thus the anomalies have a shorter average path length than the normal instances.

3.1   Training Stage

For a given dataset $X \subset R^d$, X' is a subsample of size ψ from the dataset X. Then X' is used to build a dTree.

Let T be an internal node of a dTree. Let T_l be the left child of the node T, and let T_r be the right child of the Node T. All instances in the node T constitute a distribution S.

Then the splitting of the node is described as follows. Firstly, k attributes are randomly selected to form a k-dimensional subspace when the node is split. Then the Mahalanobis distance between each instance x and the distribution S are calculated according Eq. (4), where parameters μ and Σ are the mean and covariance matrix of the distribution, respectively.

$$D_M(x, S) = \sqrt{(x - \mu)^T \Sigma^{-1} (x - \mu)} \tag{4}$$

The Mahalanobis distance was proposed by Mahalanobis in [9]. The Mahalanobis distance takes into account the correlation of the data and can be used to calculate the distance between a sample and a distribution. Also, the Mahalanobis distance is scale-invariant. And it is widely used in cluster analysis and classification techniques [10]. The Mahalanobis distance can be used for anomaly detection [11]. A instance may be anomaly if it has a large Mahalanobis distance from the distribution. In this paper, the Mahalanobis distance is used to distinguish between the possible anomalies and the normal instances in the subspace.

If the Mahalanobis distance between an instance $x_i (i = 1, 2, \ldots, n)$ and distribution S is less than p, it is divided into left child. Otherwise it is divided into right child. In other words, in the feature space, the place where the Mahalanobis distance is equal to p constitutes a hyperellipsoid. The data inside the hyperellipsoid are divided into the left child, and the data outside the hyperellipsoid are divided into the right child. In some cases, such as too few instances or coplanar instances, the covariance matrix may be singular. In this case, the Mahalanobis distance is replaced by the Euclidean distance.

$$T_l : \{x_i : D_M(x_i, S) \leq p, i = 1, 2, \ldots, n\} \tag{5}$$

$$T_r : \{x_i : D_M(x_i, S) > p, i = 1, 2, \ldots, n\} \tag{6}$$

To determine the threshold p, a parameter v is introduced. The meaning of the parameter v is the ratio of the data divided into the left child in all data. The sample divided into the left child is floor $(v \times n)$ samples with a smaller Mahalanobis distance.

When the value of k is 1, only one attribute is randomly selected at each node. At this time, it is equivalent to determining an interval on an attribute, the instances within the interval are divided into left child, and the instances outside the interval are divided into right child. The details of building a dTree are described in Algorithms 1 and 2.

The node of dTree recursively splits according to the above process until one of the following stop conditions is satisfied:

(1) Only two instances remain in the node. At this point, the two instances have the same Mahalanobis distance, so it is not necessary to divide the node again.
(2) The data in the node are the same on the selected attributes.
(3) The height of the dTree reaches the limit height. Like iTree, each dTree does not need to grow completely. The main reason is that most of the anomalies can reach the leaf nodes after being divided by several subspaces. Thus, the height of the tree can be limited to save training and test time.

dForest build an ensemble of dTree. Through the above introduction, it can be known that the construction of dForest needs to determine three parameters, namely the number of trees t, the subsampling size ψ, and the ratio v.

Number of trees t controls the ensemble size. For iForest, the path length generally converges at $t = 100$. And because dForest's node division is more purposeful, it generally converges faster than iForest. As shown in Fig. 1, the average path length tends to stabilize as the number of trees increases.

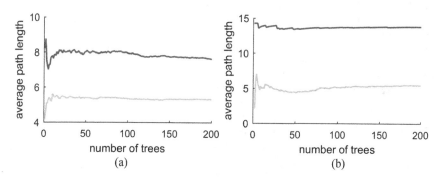

Fig. 1. The convergence curve of average path length. The blue line represents the convergence curve of a normal instance. The red line represents the convergence curve of an anomaly. In subgraph (a), the value of parameter v is 0.7. In subgraph (b), the value of parameter v is 0.9. The average path lengths converge when the number of trees is approximately 50. (Color figure online)

Parameter subsampling size ψ controls the number of training samples to build a dTree. In general, choosing a small value for this parameter can achieve same results as a large value in most datasets. The reasonable range of ψ is 32 to 256 through experimental evaluation.

Algorithm 1: dForest(X,t,ψ,v)

Inputs: X – input data, t – number of trees, ψ – subsampling size, v - ratio of the data divided into the left child

Output: a set of dTrees

1.   Initialize Forest
2.   **for** it = 1to t
3.   X'←sample(X, ψ)
4.   Forest←Forest ∪ dTree(X',v)
5.   **end for**
6.   **return** forest

Algorithm 2: dTree(X',v)

Inputs: X' - input data, v - ratio of the data divided into the left child

Output: a dTree

1.   **if** X Meet the stop condition **then**
2.   **return** exNode{Size←|X'|}
3.   **else**
4.   let Q be a list of attributes in X'
5.   randomly select the dimension k of the subspace
6.   randomly select k attributes $q \in Q$
7.   calculate the covariance matrix Σ and mean μ of X' on the attribute q
8.   **if** rank(Σ) == k:
9.   flag ← 1
10.   calculate the Mahalanobis distance D between each instance and X'
11.   **else**
12.   flag ← 0
13.   calculate the Euclidean distance D between each instance and X'
14.   **end if**
15.   sort D in ascending order
16.   let the split point p be the value of D at floor(length(X') × v)
17. X_l←filter(X',D ≤ p)
18. X_r←filter(X',D > p)
19.   **return** inNode{   Left←dTree(X_l,v),
20.   Right←dTree(X_r,v),
21.   SplitAtt←q,
22.   SplitValue←p,
23.   covMatrix←Σ,
24.   mean←μ,
25.   distType←flag}
26.   **end if**

Ratio v is used to control the proportion of left child data after division. The data of the left child are the instances inside the hyperellipsoid, and the right child contain the instances outside the hyperellipsoid. The value of the parameter v should be greater than 0.5, so as to ensure that the average path length of the normal points and the anomalies is discriminative. When training with normal instances and anomalies, a smaller v should be set. Because the distribution estimate may not be accurate, smaller v is more robust to anomalies. Through experiments, it is found that a suitable range is

[0.7,1). When training with only normal samples, the edge of the distribution are treated as the locations where anomalies may appear. Since the distribution estimation is relatively accurate at this time, a large value of v works better. Figure 1 shows the position where the average path length converges with different parameter v.

3.2 Test Stage

The proposed method uses the same way of calculating the path length and score as iForest. Consistent with iForest, anomalies will be easier to reach leaf nodes than normal instances in dForest. After combining the results of different trees, the average path length of the anomalies is usually smaller than the normal instances.

Algorithm 3 describes how to calculate the path length of a test instance on a dTree. Since the conditions for early stop are set during the training process, the size of data in many leaf nodes is greater than 1. In order to make the result comparable, the path length are adjusted. The strategy is to add c(T.size) to the path length e. The calculation method of c(T.size) is as shown in Eq. (1).

After the average path length is obtained, the score of the test instance can be calculated according to the Eq. (3). The score ranges from 0 to 1. The closer the score is to 1, the more likely the instance is to be an anomaly. The closer the score is to 0, the more likely the instance is to be normal.

Algorithm 3: PathLength(x,T,hlim,e)

Inputs: x - an instance, T - a dTree, hlim - height limit, e - current path length; to be initialized to zero when first called

Output: path length of x

1.   if T is an external node or $e > hlim$ **then**
2.   **return** $e + c(T.size)$
3.   **end if**
4. $a \leftarrow T.splitAtt$
5.   if distType == 1
6. $d \leftarrow \sqrt{(x - \mu)^T \Sigma^{-1}(x - \mu)}$
7.   **else**
8. $d \leftarrow \sqrt{(x - \mu)^2}$
9.   **end if**
10. **if** $d \leq T.splitValue$
11.   **return** PathLength(x,T.left,hlim,e+1)
12. **else**
13.   **return** PathLength(x,T.right,hlim,e+1)
14. **end if**

---

4 Experiment

In order to verify the performance of the proposed method, dForest and other state-of-the-art methods are compared on different datasets. First of all, our method is based on iForest, so iForest is selected as a comparison method. Secondly, isolation using nearest-neighbor ensembles (iNNE) is another isolation-based anomaly detection method [15]. And iNNE has shown excellent performance on many datasets. Finally, Local Outlier Factor is a well-known anomaly detection method. And LOF performs well in detecting local anomalies, and it is widely used as a comparison method for anomaly detection. In addition, dForest has been performed on two modes according to whether the selected attribute is greater than 1 at each node.

Different datasets are chosen to compare the performance of these methods. Among them, the biggest dataset of network intrusion data is used in the literature [14]. The datasets Shuttle and Breastw are collected from the source [12], and the remaining datasets are the anomaly detection benchmark datasets provided by the literature [13]. Detailed information of these datasets can be found in Table 1.

Table 1. Basic information of datasets

Dataset	Number of instances	Number of attributes	Anomalies rate
Http	567497	3	0.39%
Shuttle	49097	9	7%
Pageblocks	5393	10	9.46%
Spambase	4207	57	39.91%
Cardiotocography	2114	21	22%
Pima	768	8	34.90%
Breastw	683	9	34.99%
Ionosphere	351	32	35.90%
Stamps	340	9	9.12%

Since the normal instances and anomalies are not balanced, AUC is selected as an evaluation indicator. On each dataset, each method was performed 10 times randomly. The average of results is taken as the final result. In addition, experiments are conducted in both semi-supervised and unsupervised modes.

4.1 Semi-supervised Mode

When the training data contain only normal instances, the dataset is divided as follows. 60% of the normal instances are used for training, and the remaining 40% normal instances and all anomalies are used for testing. The result is shown in Table 2.

The values of key parameters for each method are shown in Table 3. For dForest, the number of trees t is 100 and the subsampling size ψ is 128 on all datasets. The ratio v is searched. For iForest, the number of tree t is 100 on all dataset, and the subsampling size ψ on different dataset is shown in Table 3. For iNNE, the ensemble size is 100, and the subsampling size is searched in the candidate set {2,4,8,16,32,64,128}. For LOF, the parameter neighbor number k is optimized. Among the 20 candidate values of the parameter k, the parameter corresponding to the best result is selected as the final value.

Table 2. AUC performance of different methods (semi-supervised mode)

	AUC				
	dForest random k	dForest k = 1	iForest	iNNE	LOF
Http	**1.00**	**1.00**	**1.00**	**1.00**	**1.00**
Shuttle	**1.00**	**1.00**	**1.00**	0.99	**1.00**
Pageblocks	**0.94**	0.93	0.91	0.90	**0.94**
Spambase	0.83	**0.85**	0.82	0.72	0.73
Cardiotocography	**0.84**	0.83	**0.84**	**0.84**	**0.84**
Pima	0.75	0.75	0.74	**0.77**	0.72
Breastw	**0.99**	**0.99**	**0.99**	**0.99**	**0.99**
Ionosphere	**0.97**	0.95	0.92	0.95	0.95
Stamps	0.94	0.94	0.93	**0.96**	0.94

Table 3. Parameters for different methods (semi-supervised mode)

	dForest random k	dForest k = 1	iForest	iNNE	LOF
	v	v	ψ	ψ	K
Http	0.99	0.99	512	2	500
Shuttle	0.99	0.99	256	2	5
Pageblocks	0.99	0.99	128	8	30
Spambase	0.99	0.99	128	64	500
Cardiotocography	0.7	0.8	128	2	150
Pima	0.8	0.9	128	4	200
Breastw	0.99	0.99	128	2	200
Ionosphere	0.99	0.99	128	4	20
Stamps	0.99	0.99	128	8	40

As can be seen from the results in Table 2, dForest performed best in 6 datasets in a total of 9 datasets. In contrast to iForest, dForest performs better on 5 datasets and has the same result as iForest on 4 datasets. This proves the effectiveness of dForest in anomaly detection. In addition, the same parameters t and ψ are used on 9 datasets, which also proves that it is easier to set parameters for dForest.

4.2 Unsupervised Mode

In the case of unsupervised anomaly detection, the training data contain normal instances and anomalies, and it is assumed that their labels are not provided. Similarly, 60% of each dataset is used for training. The remaining 40% is used for test. The result is shown in Table 4. And the settings for the key parameters are shown in Table 5. The results show that dForest also works well in unsupervised mode.

Table 4. AUC performance of different methods (supervised mode)

	AUC				
	dForest random k	dForest k = 1	iForest	iNNE	LOF
Http	**1.00**	**1.00**	**1.00**	**1.00**	0.42
Shuttle	**1.00**	**1.00**	**1.00**	0.62	0.55
Pageblocks	**0.92**	0.90	0.89	0.90	0.91
Spambase	0.61	0.64	0.65	0.59	**0.70**
Cardiotocography	0.79	**0.81**	0.76	0.80	**0.81**
Pima	0.70	**0.72**	0.70	0.71	0.68
Breastw	**0.98**	**0.98**	**0.98**	**0.98**	0.96
Ionosphere	**0.91**	0.87	0.85	0.89	**0.91**
Stamps	0.94	0.96	0.92	**0.97**	0.94

Table 5. Parameters for different methods (supervised mode)

	dForest random k	dForest k = 1	iForest	iNNE	LOF
	v	v	ψ	ψ	K
Http	0.99	0.99	128	2	5
Shuttle	0.9	0.9	128	2	50
Pageblocks	0.9	0.9	128	16	100
Spambase	0.9	0.9	128	2	500
Cardiotocography	0.7	0.7	128	2	500
Pima	0.8	0.9	128	4	200
Breastw	0.7	0.9	128	2	200
Ionosphere	0.8	0.99	128	8	20
Stamps	0.8	0.8	128	4	150

A comparison of the results of Tables 2 and 4 can lead to such a conclusion. Generally, training with normal instances achieves the same or better results than training with both normal and anomalous instances. The reason for this result is that the estimation of the distribution will be more accurate without anomalies. In the semi-supervised mode, it is only necessary to regard the position far from the local distribution as the position where the anomalies may lie. Therefore, a larger v is selected. In unsupervised mode, normal instances and anomalous instances are distinguished in each subspace. Moreover, the anomalous instances interfere with the estimation of the distribution, and a smaller v can make the division more robust.

In terms of time complexity, when the value of k is 1, dForest and iForest have the same time complexity. The time complexity of the training stage is $O(t\Psi\log\psi)$, and the time complexity of the test stage is $O(nt\log\psi)$. At this point, iForest and dForest are faster than other methods. When the value of k is greater than 1, the time complexity increases, but the time consuming is still within a reasonable range.

4.3   The Influence of the Ensemble Size and Subsampling Size

In the above experiment, the same value are set for the parameters ensemble size and subsampling size in dForest. Below we explore the impact of these two parameters. In iForest and iNNE, these parameters also need to be set, so they are used as a comparison. On the Pageblocks dataset, these methods are compared. The ensemble size varies from 10 to 200, and the subsampling size ranges from 4 to 2048. The result is shown in Fig. 2. As can be seen from the results, when the ensemble size reaches a certain level, dForest tends to be stable. And dForest is also robust to the choice of the sampling size. A small subsampling size can achieve better results than a large value. When the subsampling size is too large, the difference between the dTrees is small, and the performance may be degraded. The reasonable range is [32, 256].

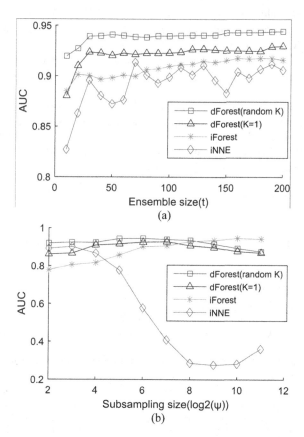

Fig. 2. The influence of the ensemble size and subsampling size. Subgraph (a) shows the effect of the ensemble size, and subgraph (b) shows the effect of the subsampling size on performance.

5 Conclusion

In this paper, we propose a new anomaly detection method, namely dForest. The main contributions of the proposed method are as follows. (1) dForest makes full use of the multi-dimensional information. dForest treats each node of the dTree as a subspace. Different combinations of randomly selected attributes form different subspaces. (2) dForest uses local distribution to distinguish between anomalous and normal instances. In dForest, the node is divided according to the distribution of local area. The instances inside the hyperellipsoid determined by the Mahalanobis distance are divided into left child, and the rest instances are divided into right child. (3) dForest has an intuitive and clear explanation. The data are continuously projected onto different subspaces, and the normal and abnormal instances are continuously distinguished in the subspace.

Experimental evaluation illustrates dForest performs well in both semi-supervised and unsupervised mode. Compared to LOF, iForest and iNNE, dForest achieves competitive AUC on different datasets. When the number of selected attributes is 1, dForest has a linear time complexity and low memory cost while achieving relatively high detection precision. Therefore, dForest can be applied to the large-scale data.

Acknowledgement. This work is partially supported by the Natural Science Foundation of Tianjin (No.18ZXZNGX00200), the National Key Research and Development Program of China (2016YFC0400709), the Science and Technology Commission of Tianjin Binhai New Area (BHXQKJXM-PT-ZJSHJ-2017005), the Natural Science Foundation of Tianjin (18YFYZC G00060) and Nankai University (91922299).

References

1. Chandola, V., Banerjee, A., Kumar, V.: Anomaly detection: a survey. ACM Comput. Surv. **41**(3), 1–58 (2009)
2. He, Z., Xu, X., Deng, S.: Discovering cluster-based local outliers. Pattern Recogn. Lett. **24** (9–10), 1641–1650 (2003)
3. Breunig, M.M., Kriegel, H.P., Ng, R.T.: LOF: identifying density-based local outliers. In: ACM SIGMOD International Conference on Management of Data. ACM (2000)
4. Knorr, E.M., Ng, R.T., Tucakov, V.: Distance-based outliers: algorithms and applications. VLDB J. **8**(3–4), 237–253 (2000)
5. Liu, F.T., Kai, M.T., Zhou, Z.H.: Isolation forest. In: Eighth IEEE International Conference on Data Mining (2009)
6. Liu, F.T., Ting, K.M., Zhou, Z.H.: Isolation-based anomaly detection. ACM Trans. Knowl. Discov. Data **6**(1), 1–39 (2012)
7. Scholkopf, B.: Estimating the support of a high-dimensional distribution. Neural Comput. **13** (7), 1443–1471 (2014)
8. Williams, G., Baxter, R., He, H., Hawkins, S., Gu, L.: A comparative study of RNN for outlier detection in data mining. In: Proceedings of 2002 IEEE International Conference on Data Mining, ICDM 2003. IEEE (2002)
9. Mahalanobis, P.C.: On the generalised distance in statistics. Proc. Natl. Inst. Sci. India **12**, 49–55 (1936)

10. Maesschalck, R.D., Jouan-Rimbaud, D., Massart, D.L.: The Mahalanobis distance. Chemometr. Intell. Lab. Syst. **50**(1), 1–18 (2000)
11. Patil, N., Das, D., Pecht, M.: Anomaly detection for IGBTs using Mahalanobis distance. Microelectron. Reliab. **55**(7), 1054–1059 (2015)
12. Dua, D., Karra Taniskidou, E.: UCI Machine Learning Repository. School of Information and Computer Science, University of California, Irvine, CA (2017). http://archive.ics.uci.edu/ml
13. Yamanishi, K., Takeuchi, J.I., Williams, G., Milne, P.: On-line unsupervised outlier detection using finite mixtures with discounting learning algorithms. Data Min. Knowl. Discov. **8**(3), 275–300 (2004)
14. Swersky, L., Marques, H.O., Sander, J., Campello, R.J.G.B., Zimek, A.: On the evaluation of outlier detection and one-class classification methods. In: IEEE International Conference on Data Science & Advanced Analytics. IEEE (2016)
15. Bandaragoda, T.R., Ting, K.M., Albrecht, D., Liu, F.T., Zhu, Y., Wells, J.R.: Isolation-based anomaly detection using nearest-neighbor ensembles. Comput. Intell. **34**, 968–998 (2018)

Author Index

Bai, Gang   135

Chen, Biao   135
Chen, Xiaobing   15, 27, 55

Du, Weijian   27, 55

Gao, Yingqi   96
Gong, Lei   3
Gu, Jianan   109
Guo, Song   96

Jin, Luyang   55

Kang, Hong   96

Li, Siyang   43
Li, Tao   96
Liang, Yun   71
Liu, Shaoli   15, 55
Lou, Wenqi   3
Lu, Ye   123
Lu, Youyou   43

Ma, Xiaoqing   135

Ning, Zhong   86

Pei, Songwen   86
Peng, Shaohui   55

Shen, Tianma   86
Shu, Jiwu   43
Song, Jin   15, 55

Wang, Chao   3
Wang, Kai   96
Wang, Longhua   43
Wang, Lulu   86
Wang, Zhi   123
Weng, Chuliang   109
Wu, Linyang   27

Xie, Jiaming   71
Xie, Kunpeng   96, 123
Xie, Xueshuo   123

Yang, Fan   43
Yao, Chengfei   135

Zhang, Lin   123
Zhang, Yujun   123
Zhao, Xiaosong   135
Zheng, Beilei   109
Zhi, Tian   15, 27, 55
Zhou, Xuehai   3
Zhuang, Yimin   15, 27, 55